The Well Church Book

The Well Church Book

BROWNE BARR

For Beth and Stan

with unbounded gratitude
for the grace of your
sustaining friendship.

B

A CROSSROAD BOOK
The Seabury Press · New York

December 1976

The Seabury Press
815 Second Avenue
New York, N.Y. 10017

Printed in the United States of America

Library of Congress Cataloging in Publication Data

Barr, Browne.   The well church book.
"A Crossroad book."
1. Church renewal—Addresses, essays, lectures.
2. Church—Addresses, essays, lectures. I. Title.
BV600.2.B36   262'.001   76-18291   ISBN 0-8164-0304-X

To our littlest flock

Virginia and George
Kathryn and Maureen

John

Maurice

Holli and Paul
Cassie

"God setteth the solitary in families. . . ."
Psalm 68

. . . Tend that flock of God whose
shepherds you are, and do it, not under
compulsion, but of your own free will,
as God would have it; not for gain but
out of sheer devotion; not tyrannizing
over those who are allotted to your care,
but setting an example to the flock.

I Peter 5:1–4 (NEB)

Acknowledgments

Portions of this book have been delivered as lectures at Chicago Theological Seminary, Princeton Institute of Theology, the University of Dubuque, and in various other schools and convocations of the church from Montana to Florida and home again. Indeed, a few paragraphs here and there may have been heard at Emory University, and Duke University, too; and certainly some of them have emerged more than once in the congregation which I know and love the most, the First Congregational Church of Berkeley, California, to whom I am indebted for any practical wisdom which may grace these pages and whose life is spread out here for everyone to see—all of it, save a few warts!

My indebtedness to individual persons is so deep and so embarrassingly vast that I hesitate to mention anyone by name. Indeed, the lay persons quoted here and there in these pages often represent an unnamed company to whom they are indebted as am I. "Need I say more? Time is too short for me to tell the stories of Gideon, Barak, Samson, and Jephtha," of Mary, Albert, John and Boyard, of Della and Cordelia, and especially of my former colleague, the Reverend Fred Strasburg of St. Paul, Minnesota, who suggested the theme for the Princeton assignment and thus provided focus for the concerns subsequently developed in these pages. Finally, credit for the title goes to Henrietta, the cat.

Browne Barr

Berkeley
New Year's Day 1976

Contents

Introduction:
New Heart, New Being

Sometimes we forget that Karl Barth was expressing a Christian reality which will not lie down and die when he said:

> Take good note, that a parson who does not believe that in this congregation of his, including those men and women, old wives and children, Christ's own congregation exists, does not believe at all in the existence of the Church. *Credo ecclesiam* means that I believe that here, at this place, in the visible assembly, the work of the Holy Spirit takes place.[1]

The reality of the church is "in this congregation of his" and the quality of life and experience in that congregation can scarcely be exaggerated. Fortunately, that quality and experience is not all up to *us*. It is still the work of the Holy Spirit. But that does not mean that there is nothing we can do to prepare a way in the wilderness of ordinary congregations for them to be more hospitable to that Divine force.

It may indeed be true that "ordinary congregations" are doomed, that they need more than a new heart if they are to have new being. It may be that nothing short of a revolutionary change of the Body itself will do to free up the work of the Holy Spirit in and through the churches. Yet even if the traditional parish church has no future, even if the age of a new *diaspora* is upon us as Karl Rahner proposes, Chris-

---

1. *Dogmatics in Outline,* trans. G. T. Thomson (London: SCM Press, 1949), p. 145.

tian *community* of some sort remains and will be even more important to the individual believer when the church is disestablished and dispersed and there is little Christian affirmation in the world at large. So Rahner writes that in such a future

. . . there will be Christian communities all over the world, though not evenly distributed. Everywhere they will be a *little* flock. . . .[2]

That "little flock," established or dispersed, on Main Street or underground, is the concern of this book.

The term "little flock" has a tender and sentimental feeling to it with which the descendents of Descartes or Kant have difficulty. Indeed, their difficulty, reflected in much "liberal" Protestant theology of the twentieth century, may have helped create the void in the churches to which this volume is addressed. The "feeling" quality of that term, "little flock," is quite consistent with the "new heart" local churches need because it has to do with the emotional quality of life. That feeling or emotion must not be obscured by or confused with sentimentality. Sentimentality, Ernest Hemingway is reputed to have said, is an "emotion you don't have to pay for." The new heart which characterizes the new being in the local church is nurtured by emotions which we do have to pay for, which do have costly and creative consequences.

The drive for social justice which has characterized the greatest reformers has behind it great emotions, profound experience at the feeling level. The night word came of the assassination of Martin Luther King, Jr., one of the black members of our congregation called me to go with him to a meeting in the black community "to reason together." Soon the "reasoning" and planning gave way to mourning and praying. At last someone said to a singer, "Sing the song he loved." I expected the man who rose would sing "We Shall Overcome." He did not. Slowly there sounded in our midst, "Precious Lord, take my hand . . ."

So also with the missionary impulse of the church: the energy for it, the drive behind it, is never primarily intellectual, but emotional. So

2. Karl Rahner, *Mission and Grace,* trans. Cecily Hastings (London: Sheed & Ward, 1963), p. 25.

with effective Christian education and evangelism. Public worship which binds a congregation together in a great Te Deum and renews and refreshes the individual Christian is experienced primarily at the feeling level. The practical support which comes in time of trouble has its primary meaning not at the practical level but in the life of feeling.

We need make no apology then for concern for sentiment and emotion. There are many books about church renewal which seek accreditation primarily in the intellectual life of the church but that is not broad nor deep enough to touch the affliction besetting many ordinary congregations. A *new heart and the ensuing new being* for the little flock will come at the feeling level of life; it will endure and be fruitful, however, only if it is protected by a *reasonable* theology consistent with the biblical witness. Works abound on that reasonable theology, with particular emphasis on the reasonable part; this work seeks to build on such a theology but with emphasis on the actual life within the community of faith.

Somewhere long since forgotten I read that every person needs "a little parish of the heart," a surrounding group of loving persons where one experiences a depth of life, tender and renewing, nowhere else to be had. That is another way of expressing the human need to be part of a "little flock." When I read that I thought to myself, "That is it! That is what my church is to me!" I do not believe it is that to me *because* I am the minister but really in spite of it. There, in that company, I feel secure and warm and rebuked and renewed and directed.

That *is* really true for me. There in the local church is my "little parish of the heart," a very particular and special community, larger than my family but smaller than my town. It is a very crucial constellation of persons which I feel I could not live without. I have inquired among many persons I know in that community of faith and I have found many of them feeling much the same.

Yet, alas! It is not so for everyone. It is even not so for other persons of our own families of flesh and blood who also belong to churches and are faithful to their responsibilities within them. My concern and curiosity about what makes the difference sparked these pages. That difference came dramatically to mind when I counted up the funerals in my immediate family in the past few years: my mother, my two brothers, a sister-in-law and a brother-in-law—all church members. I was appalled to realize that not one of those funerals was held in a church.

My sister and sister-in-law each told me on the separate occasion of their bereavement that it would be "too hard" to hold the funerals for their husbands in the church. I did not press the argument. It was hardly the time or circumstance and I was not unacquainted with the pressures upon them and a long tradition of "services" in a mortuary chapel.

It was too late to bear witness to them that on many an occasion the funeral in our church of one of its members had been a time of most profound and reinforcing Christian experience. That experience was related in a very significant way to the fact that the service was held *in* the church building, *in the place* of many other memories and many other hopes, a circumstance which we shall explore in detail in Chapter V. The healing quality of such services is related significantly to the feeling about a building, a feeling which is frequently corrupted into building-worship but doesn't need to be. I can recall services, even in the event of tragic deaths, yes, especially then, when the community of faith including the most intimately bereft has been lifted up in that place by the Spirit as at no other time, and as would be virtually impossible as guests or patrons in a mortuary chapel. As the casket has been borne down the aisle and the gathered "friends in Christ" have sung, "For All the Saints,"

> We feebly struggle,
> They in glory shine—
> Yet all are one in Thee
> For all are Thine,

the Comforter has surrounded us and the doxologies have been divinely inspired and we have discovered what it can mean to find one's life renewed in "the little parish of the heart."

Philip Slater's provocative book *The Pursuit of Loneliness* was recommended to me by a member of our parish. It is subtitled, "American Culture at the Breaking Point." Slater contends that one human desire deeply and uniquely frustrated by our Western culture is "the desire for *community*—the wish to live in trust and fraternal cooperation with one's fellows in a total and visible collective entity."

The local church gathered in a beloved and accustomed place of worship and prayer for a Christian funeral can be one instance of "trust and fraternal cooperation . . . in a total and visible collective entity." To help ordinary local churches move in this direction in every aspect of their lives from church suppers and church fights to world mission and great funerals for ordinary people should command the energy of Christian leadership in Western society. The church has an opportunity to become such a community—but more! It possesses crucial attributes which no purely human community can supply.

Not long ago a colorful and attractively designed and worded invitation came to me in the mail. It was an invitation to join an "alternative community." This community was described as "on-going" and "open-ended," composed of "diverse people united by openness to growth and change." It promised "mutual emotional support" and "to bring new life to all your (other) commitments" and an opportunity "to become change agents in society."

In every way it sounded like the ideal parish church except in the very first sentence, which was intended, I suspect, as an attractive declaration of freedom. "This is a community," the brochure read, "with no human restrictions or qualifications except for our common humanity." So there at the outset this beautiful, idealistic, and hopeful community was declared free of the distinguishing qualification of the church: its transcendental characteristic. In every other aspect it affirmed what the existential church should be, a community of loving acceptance, personal liberation, and public effectiveness.

We have many such loving and useful communities trying to be born. They address themselves to the loneliness which permeates urban America and to the sense of powerlessness felt by individuals in our complex society. They often seek to find their life in a rustic setting with a sentimental flashback to Walden Pond overlooking the truth that, if the rural garden is an instance of the human capacity to transform the wilderness, the city is even more so. Indeed, it is only the city with its libraries, museums, hospitals, galleries, universities, and concert halls which provides that intensification of life that is the gift of civilization.

So these communities in both rural and urban settings struggle for life. Some appear to develop self-consciously and others are apparently born spontaneously in response to this profound human longing. However they come into being, their lives have been almost uniformly short, difficult to sustain, easily lost in that "common humanity" which is their boasted single qualification. Such communities with practical idealism about meeting genuine human need nevertheless fail with predictable regularity. Their goals appear good and sound, but there is something too flimsy about their foundation and too shallow about their resources for inner reinforcement.

On the other hand, the local church somehow keeps on going through all sorts of strain and trouble. But we often have reason to wonder if persistence is the only virtue it possesses ("a thousand years the same") because it so often fails to articulate, much less fulfill, the need for "mutual emotional support," nor does it bring new life to its members, much less help them to be "agents for social change." It often just stumbles along, judging and being judged, but seldom collapsing altogether.

Can its endurability lie in the fact that it does possess some restrictions and qualification far beyond "our common humanity"? In that it differs from most proposed alternative communities, possessed as most of them are by a sentimental view of human freedom, unacquainted with, and hence unprepared for, the profound dimensions of human sin. It differs from the dominant optimistic culture of Western society by familiarity with the dark themes in human experience. It is restricted and qualified and hence immeasurably liberated by loyalty to a common and crucified Lord who in turn defines and redeems our common humanity. Much has been written on this subject. It is the substance of Christian theology and lies at the heart of all discussion about the church. "The Church's one foundation is Jesus Christ her Lord." To be sure! But with that impressive foundation how can local churches do something more than demonstrate the capacity to endure?

This book proposes six characteristics—not exclusively but suggestively—which will be increasingly evident in any Christian parish as it finds a new heart and a new being. These characteristics are suggested in the chapter titles. The primary concern of those chapters is not to reexamine the theological foundation of the church, although that foundation will be implicit all the way along. Without it we cannot reason together, as is our purpose, about helping local churches *become* warm and beautiful and effective human communities. But it is that practical and urgent "becoming," the stirring of new heart in Barth's "visible assembly," which will occupy our primary attention. The first three chapters weigh in heavily on the practical. I even risk some actual, concrete, specific suggestions—and not only about funerals! The last three chapters have more theological reflection, which I hope will tend to reinforce the most important parts of the earlier chapters. All six of them will be greatly enriched and focused and brought to practical usefulness as local congregations use them to reflect on their life together and open themselves to new promptings of the Holy Spirit.

O Little Flock, take heart! for through the whole work I wish to press upon you, with all the sweet reasonableness I can command, my earnest conviction that the local churches of the Western world possess incredible potential. They possess resources fully adequate to rescue persons in our society from the frustrations which are suffocating them and to deliver our civilization from the corruptions which can destroy it. Such creative enterprising neither begins nor ends in the top echelons of either church or state. Its vitality and power is in the quality of life in local communities. All across Christendom are these "religious collectives" called parish churches supposedly concerned with the quality of that life and designed to channel vitality and power quite beyond our common humanity. They have everything going for them in the way of foundation, a long history, a profound tradition, a liberating book, a saving secret for dealing with sin, a Torah that is both law and story, so they don't disappear like yesterday's commune. Nonetheless, many of them seem never able to take off, to get going, to build a contemporary and beautiful structure of human persons on that splendid "given" foundation. This volume hopes to give some boost and encouragement to any little flock eager for new heart and new being.

If it seems, except for the last chapter, that we are too much concerned about the inner life of the church rather than its work in the world, that is a deliberate decision. There are many excellent books concerned with the life of the church in the world. But, like persons, until we get our own "heads together," as they say, we are not very effective in helping others do the same. Surely it will be evident before the last page that the "little flock" can never get its "head together" until its new heart is lost in its work of creative love in the world. Hence, a new heart begets a new being.

·I·

Where There Is
Love Like Christ's

I suspect some early Christian, concerned with giving hope and encouragement to Christians in Asia Minor, was seeking to nurture a congregation when he urged the people in the church at Ephesus:

> Be generous to one another, tender-hearted, forgiving one another as God in Christ forgave you. In a word, as God's dear children, try to be like Him, and live in love as Christ loved you . . . .

Well, that sounds like the sort of sentimental encouragement one has come to expect from preachers when they approach the problem of human relationships—long on religion and short on reality, long on forgiveness and tender-heartedness and short on practical ways to make the experience of self-worth real in daily life.

But that is to underestimate the counsel from Ephesians. It plunges a bit deeper and more realistically than a superficial reading of it suggests. It recognizes that everyone possesses the creative power to effect change in other persons. We say of one friend, she always makes me feel uncomfortable, or of another, he always makes me feel good. When we go to a party or to work, or even plunge into freeway traffic, considerate people should take seriously their own creative capacity to effect change in others through the ordinary and casual exchanges of the day.

In a generally helpful book entitled *Peoplemaking* and intended as a workbook to help families find better ways of living together, Virginia Satir lists four qualities which she has consistently discovered in families whose homes are interesting and rewarding places to be. In working with countless families she has learned that the families which appear to possess the greatest capacities to be centers of vitality and nurturing for their members usually possess these four qualities.

The first quality which Ms. Satir discovered almost universally in families which were nurturing and vital was a *high sense of self-worth among the members*. They enabled each member of the family to have a good personal feeling, a high sense of self-worth. But that is easier said than done. It involves some deeply fundamental feelings about life and purpose and other people and one's own gifts, health, age, appearance. High self-esteem grows in a particular atmosphere and flourishes in a particular environment. The local church is ideally constituted to be such an environment.

John Macquarrie reminds us that to be like God is "to have the capacity for letting-be, for conferring being." We share God's creative power. We can use it, if we will, to build up the self-esteem of others, especially those with whom we are most intimately associated, who look to us for support or always find us close by in life's personal relationships.

Christians may call to mind the doctrines of the faith which undergird and support such attitudes, not only that persons are made in the image of God but that God's self-disclosure in Christ overflows with caring for persons of all kinds, with special and focused attention on those with good reason to feel a very low level of self-esteem: the hungry, the naked, the sick, the imprisoned. Christ comes in them! He is cared for when they are cared for. How better can their self-worth be dramatized. But in many churches all this remains frozen in the Bible as lifeless dogma or to be demonstrated only to those quite *outside* the local church in dramatic missionary effort overseas or brave social action in the seamy streets and back corners of the world.

Of course, it *is* in the Bible and it *is* dogma and it *is* to be demonstrated in a wide outreach to an alienated world. But it is *also* to be demonstrated at our own doorstep and in our own congregations and families. The local church, exercising the priesthood of all believers, should be a primary place for this mutuality which "confers being," which can help set free in all people good feelings about themselves. Sometimes it appears in very simple guise. A mature woman who deeply regrets that she hates to sew because she suspects she might really have a talent for it reports that whenever she put in a hem as a child and took it to her mother for inspection, all her mother ever commented about were the puckers. She never seemed to see all the rest of the hem which by precious effort small hands had managed to get to lie flat. So in many a little family—from nuclear families to professional associations—we find it easier, only natural (original sin?), to see the puckers and ignore the achievement. But in the church such perpetual fault-finding is not simply a minor vice, it is a spiritual crime; it kills the spirit which can transform an ordinary group of persons into Christ's little flock. Careful appreciation of the best in one another, drawing it out and affirming one another in that fashion, is to be nurturing and supportive; it is to love like Christ, creatively, conferring being, bringing something new and beautiful into the light of day.

This conferring is not the sole prerogative of older persons, a gift which age develops so senior persons can help the younger ones coming along. It applies across the board. It is a gift which older people need quite as much as younger ones. In our church we are exploring the conviction that the last stage of life (for those persons given three score years and more) possesses particular beauty and usefulness all its own. "The Search for Growth and Meaning Seminar" has no ceiling on the age requirement, but a floor. You must be sixty-five. The community of faith is just beginning to rediscover the particular beauty and promise of age, and every member of the church has the opportunity to help that new experience happen. It always involves raising the level of self-esteem.

Margaret Mead writes appreciatively of her good fortune in being able "to look up to my parents' minds well past my own middle years. And I watched my father grow, shed his earlier racial prejudices and come to respect new institutions of the Federal Government, such as Social Security. . . . Watching a parent grow," she concludes, "is one of the most reassuring experiences anyone can have." Can you guess what it may have meant to that man to sense his daughter's increasing appreciation of him?

A most readable and encouraging book by D. D. Stonecypher, Jr., M.D., entitled *Getting Older and Staying Young,* enlarges on a principle which the author calls the Law of Aging: "Those functions (physical or mental) which are exercised tend to persist. Those which are not exercised tend to disappear." [1] Regular and normal interaction of older persons with younger persons where each accepts the other as a person is an ideal environment for the exercise of all human capacities. Age and youth are natural working partners in countless local churches.

The local church is ideally situated for that teaming up and also for the delight and surprise of intergenerational affairs which can often be a prelude to more profound mutual appreciation. Recently a "happening" of delight for all ages in our parish was experienced through an "Intergenerational Hop" in the assembly hall. Popular dances from every era for the past one hundred years were promised. Everyone was invited to come in clothes like the ones he wore in high school. Plenty of chairs were promised for spectators. The walls were decorated with priceless copies of old sheet music and the evening was filled with waltzes and the Charleston, jitter-bugging and the two-step, square dances and reels, and dimly lighted cheek-to-cheek dances of World War II. The following Sunday morning the gray-heads and the long-hairs discovered they had "conferred being" upon each other: friendship, understanding, increased self-esteem.

In more sober and more substantial fashion another group of younger persons in our church, "turned on" by new interest in weaving and other handcrafts, remembered older people in the parish who had skills along these lines. They were worried by the thought that those skills might be lost altogether in another ten or fifteen years if they didn't learn them. So they approached some older people who had almost come to believe that there was nothing they could do that younger people couldn't do more efficiently and faster with some new method or gadget which only intimidated them. What a transforming day it was when these older people discovered that they were sought

1. New York: W. W. Norton, 1974; p. 26.

out because of a unique skill they possessed and others treasured! Older people and younger people and all other people grow when someone in the little flock nurtures their self-esteem with appreciation, "confers being." "Be generous to one another . . . live in love as Christ loved you."

As much as the little flock must be concerned with helping its older members to their full share of high self-esteem, those older persons themselves would be the first to press the question, "But what about the children?" That is a primary question. Unfortunately some parishes have become so child-centered that churchgoing is seen as a children's activity, but perhaps that is better than putting children out of sight altogether in a segregated ghetto called "the Church School." The opportunity which the Christian community of faith possesses in this precise moment in human history to raise the lifelong level of self-esteem for children may be unprecedented.

Kenneth Keniston, professor of psychology at Yale and director of the Carnegie Council on Children, argues convincingly that "for 200 years Americans have valued the child mainly as a producer—first on the farm, then in the factory and now as a cognitive whiz." When he says that this ethic of productivity has promoted the virtues of "industry, labor, self-discipline, persistence and thrift," he strikes near home for many an American Protestant parent who views sound religion as an ally of these personal character traits. Although that same parent would never put her child out to work long hours in the factory for the benefit of the family, she is the vigorous supporter of a system which pressures the child to do well in school and in competition and especially in the College Board examinations. Thus the child is still primarily seen as a potential "producer." Only now it is his cognitive ability which is prized and promoted. We have simply moved from valuing a strong back for the farm to nimble hands for the factory, to a sharp mind for science, industry, and commerce.

If concern with the self-esteem of all its members is truly a cornerstone of a church which would approach its potential as a little flock of Christ, then the self-esteem of the smallest child is crucial. Keniston might well be addressing every local church in its entirety and not only the Children's Committee or Church School Board or whatever other group we set up to make it easier for the whole church to bypass responsibility for the future of its children.

When we play the cognitive game, as Keniston makes clear, those who play it well play it at the expense of other human qualities which, he suspects, "are, in God's eyes, far more important: morality, kindness, feeling, joy, imagination, playfulness, grace, artistic ability—to say nothing of love. And the price paid by those at the bottom is all too well known—children who by the second grade have accepted the label of 'losers' and who carry it with them forever." [2] He says that their alternative vision at the Carnegie Council "is still vague, but some of its components are clear. It is a vision of a society which, without deprecating work, would place equal emphasis on other human qualities such as love, care, compassion, grace and imagination." Well, the Carnegie Council may have to wait a long time to see the vision implemented widely in American society. But the local parish church already has a grip on it. That grip could be immeasurably strengthened within months through the immediate, direct, and specific leadership of a single concerned person—especially the effort of the parish's most highly honored elder, trustee, or deacon. The effectiveness of that person would be incredibly extended in influence if the minister, and sexton too, were also converted to the same point of view. The entire group must participate in a deliberate design to increase the self-esteem of every child, not only those gifted with high I.Q.'s and fluent speech.

So also in the growing awareness of women as a "put-down" group in society, the church must be open and listen and counsel together about how to confer new being on hurting persons. Hear this paragraph written by an attractive, talented young mother in our parish:

> I can't speak for men; I can only speak for myself and some women whose words, written and spoken, I've heard. Many women have over a great deal of time carried considerable baggage—felt themselves to be inadequate, never quite accepted, never quite acceptable, never quite measuring up. The whole culture tells us we're either too ugly, too awkward, too stupid, too inarticulate, too talkative, too domineering, too weak (take your choice!)—and besides, what we do is less important

2. Yale Alumni magazine (April 1974), p. 10.

than what men do. Our culture equates worth with productivity, which is often measured in monetary terms. Somehow I feel that both men and women would be better off if we could begin to act as though we believed that *being is more important than doing.*

This young woman concluded her share of a report to a long-range planning committee with these sober and truthful words:

If the church shies away from problems affecting persons, it in effect says their problems are not important enough to deal with. If something is a problem to *someone,* it's a *problem,* and should be listened to. Listening to each other is a gift which for most of us has become rusty through little use. We need to practice *listening* and *taking each other seriously,* learning to truly *accept* each other *where we are.*

Another able woman, alerting our parish to the changing world of women, presented unassailable statistics regarding that world. For example, she reminded, or informed, that planning committee that the "average mother today has 40 years of life ahead of her after her youngest child is in school." Then she concluded:

People, of course, may have very different reactions to statistics such as these. Speaking for myself, I have found them very powerful and impelling, and I trust that it is not difficult for you to see why I hope so deeply that this community, which continues to search for new and increased ways of caring for one another, will demonstrate particular concern now for its girl children.

It is not only older people and little people and women people who can use higher self-esteem. Another one of the beautiful realities about most local churches is the presence of "characters," persons with handicaps or problems which exclude them from almost every other social relationship except their own family, if they still have one. The spirit of Christ has enough vitality in all but the most spiritually impoverished church to insist upon acceptance of such persons as persons, as dearly loved children of God. However, it is crucial that they be known as persons with names and gifts and histories and futures. When Mr. So-and-So ceases to be Mr. So-and-So in the church and becomes that "old alcoholic," the church, like the community, has conveniently made him a nonperson and thus deposed him.

In far more sophisticated fashion there is the "put down" practiced by those clergy who forget they are pastors first and psychologists second and help the church bypass difficult people by labeling them. When Mrs. X is labeled as a "passive-aggressive personality," she is made impersonal and separated from the little parish of the heart. The distinguishing characteristic of Christ's flock is seeing and knowing persons as persons, not as problems or functionaries or case studies. Every member must be held generously, tenderly, forgivingly, *by name,* as a cared-for person. Liturgically every church which practices infant baptism celebrates the person by hearing the child named and by receiving that child into the parish. How disappointing when baptism is made a private affair with no congregational participation and no care promised by the community of faith.

The beauty and richness of the baptism of infants is clouded when the congregation is absent or when its participation is minimal. Certainly, infant baptism is corrupted when the visible church does not declare its intent and purpose to be an instrument of Christ's welcome of the baptized one into his little flock. Not long ago a sermon by the Reverend Mary Eakin entitled "Windows, Doors, and Chimneys" concluded, "Eagerly and with simple trust we may turn even our newborn children toward that light and pray for them as for all God's children the gift of God's Holy Spirit to guard and guide them all their days. Amen." Then the preacher continued after a brief pause: "This declaration of the Good News moves now appropriately to the action of the sacrament. Those parents who wish to present their children for Christian baptism are invited to do so at this time." The congregation and choir remained seated and sang a baptismal hymn, a hymn of entrance, as the parents entered the main doors of the church with their children. Then the baptism took place, which includes the following participation by members of the church:

> We as members of this church affirm the baptism of these children and receive them joyously into the care of the church, thereby covenanting with you who are their parents to walk with you and to pray with you in your holy commitment to rear your child in the knowledge and love of God as that love is seen and known in Jesus Christ our Lord.

So also may the church celebrate the *person* liturgically at the time of death. In our congregation there is an annual Memorial Service. At that time the minister says: "When we speak to another the name of a distant mutual friend we discover that such speaking makes that person clearer to us and present again. So now we speak with gentle voice the names of those who have walked with us here and have in recent months joined that great company of saints in the future yet ahead. We recall their ways and find them here as their Christian names are spoken once more in this place."

Then the name of each person who has died during the past year is read from a card on which that name has been carefully printed. The card is then placed upon the Lord's Table and a prayer for the dead is offered after all the names have been read. In the careful reading of those names the congregation has experienced again the wonderful miracle of human speech to bring into the present that which is absent. (There will be more about this miracle in Chapter IV.)

Alas, how difficult it is to achieve personal support and careful intimacy in the local church, especially where the parish is large and widespread. No small part of the frustration of the ministry lies in the fact that the burden of this relationship has been centered upon the minister. This presents an obvious practical difficulty but also a subtle and often hidden psychological difficulty. In such relationships he receives all the personal affirmation which should be distributed among all the members of the parish family, helping and being helped. Even if he is sturdy enough to receive all that support, he is seldom wise or strong enough to provide it. Yet it is widely assumed that, if the members can't know and love all the members, the minister must.

Before returning to the pastorate after several years in theological education I read a book which I had long recommended to my students in a course called "Care of the Parish." The minister who wrote this book reported his system for getting acquainted personally with his entire parish of many hundreds of people. He set up an elaborate system of family calling between five-thirty and nine-thirty almost every evening of the week. It sounded great, thorough, well-organized, concentrated at an optimum time to find the whole family home. So I tried it—for about a month. I ended up helping other people with their dishes and other people's children with their homework and dealing with other people's frustrations at the weary tag end of the day. Trying to keep up that schedule, with the fatigue brought on not only by its intensity and emotional load but by the sense of guilt about the neglect of my own family, came near to sending me back to the classroom where I had given advice about pastoral care and not tried to exercise it.

Persistent and growing personal relationships cannot be just between a minister, or God forbid, a Minister of Visitation, and all the people one by one. His tenure is too uncertain, his gifts too limited, his body too finite. Effective personal caring must arise from a living and continuing "network of caring," a complex interweaving and overarching and undergirding energy of love throughout the whole little flock.

The revival of John Wesley's "classes" under the general rubric of "small groups" in the contemporary church is instructive. The earliest Methodist classes were made up of about twelve persons, each under a "class leader," charged to collect a penny weekly from each member to retire a debt on the Bristol chapel. But, aha! note the serendipity! According to a noted church historian, "Its advantages for spiritual oversight and mutual watch were soon even more apparent than its financial merits." [3] Indeed! Those classes were strong because the class leader made a substantial commitment of energy and time for a considerable length of time to the total welfare of each person in the class.

Many well-intentioned systems for dividing larger parishes into circles or colonies to make personal relationships better have failed for the lack of a well-prepared and committed corps of lay leaders. The dollars may be solicited annually but the pennies must be gone after every week! Furthermore, under considerable economic pressure competent boards or committees of stewardship in the local church insist upon training sessions for "callers" who go after the dollars, but spiritual oversight is left to intuition and good will. We need much larger commitment and much more intensive preparation to provide leadership for an ongoing parish network of caring and concern than ever proposed for even the most successful financial campaign.

---

3. Willison Walker, *A History of the Christian Church* (New York: Charles Scribner's Sons, 1920), p. 515.

Many a local church might begin tremendous growth in being Christ's little flock if at least as much organizational effort and leadership training and individual commitment were put into significant deepening of personal relationships as is given to the annual Every Member Canvass. An unrealistic burden would be lifted from the minister, the difficult financial burden and spiritual dead-end street of church professionalism (that is, "hiring the work done") would be closed down and persons could once more come into their own in a vital community of love.

The preparation and deployment of para-professionals in the church is a contemporary expression of the priesthood of all believers, much as Wesley's class leaders were a similar manifestation in 1742. In our parish we are in the first stages of such an approach. Some time ago the following advertisement ran for two weeks in our parish newsletter:

WANTED

FCCB [First Congregational Church of Berkeley] is ready to engage, without salary, lead workers for Sunburst. Time commitment: not less than 20 hours a week. Such volunteers must be open to receive appropriate instruction and guidance which will be commensurate with the responsibility to be assumed. They must be persons who have the potential to help others in groups and individually. They must be physically mobile. They must be readily accessible by telephone. They must be open to growth and change themselves and have the ability to relate warmly to others. They will be reimbursed for expenses incurred, such as travel, telephone, supplementary education. . . .

As a result of that appeal and the planning and preparation which lay behind it, six persons have been recruited in a careful and serious fashion who have committed themselves to give twenty hours a week for at least two years. The parish has been divided into six sectors and each of these persons is the leader of a sector responsible for knowing personally every member of the church in her sector. (I say "her" because the men who were interested in becoming leaders were unable to make the time commitment. The women who were enlisted varied greatly in age and background and every one of them had to make special arrangements about family or employment to accept this responsibility. A complete report, prepared by one of the lead workers to share the details of the program with other congregations appears in Appendix A.)

Each sector leader will endeavor to nourish a caring group who will join with her in practical Christian concern for all the persons in their area. This includes evangelical concern for the religiously uncommitted in that area as well as "pastoral" concern for fellow parishioners. Inasmuch as each sector radiates out from the church at the center, theoretically the whole wide world is our parish and our missionary outreach could be organized through the sectors, too.

These leaders undertook six weeks of initial mutual planning of how to tackle this task. This was followed with six weeks of intensive training, which included a crash course in the New Testament and field experience in calling. The training and weekly group prayer and consultation continues as a regular built-in part of the program. Recently two members attended a special course offered nearby in Alcohol Studies and then returned to share their experience with the group. They are now better prepared to identify an alcohol problem when they encounter it; they know local and national resources which are prepared to help with such situations; [4] further, they are resolved to urge the appropriate board in the church to present a mini-alcohol-studies program for the entire parish. Another member has recently presented a report to the entire group on the aging which grew out of her experience in concentrated calling on that group in her sector and which put reality and vitality into the extensive reading the group had done on the subject. This ongoing education of these para-professionals is reminiscent of early education for both clergy and lawyers and has much that is good going for it. It is certainly in the context of "doing."

These volunteers are volunteers! The church budget includes allowance for their actual expenses for travel, education, child care, telephone, but no stipend. Working with them takes a large part of the ministers' time but infinitely multiplies the effectiveness of the total ministry of the church. This program in our parish somehow became identified as "Sunburst." The name has stuck and increasingly it seems appropriate. Recently when discussing some transportation

4. National Clearinghouse for Information on Alcohol Abuse and Alcoholism. Box 2045, Rockville, Md. 20852.

problems with them I recalled the deaconesses in the church of my childhood. I explained how the deaconesses were welcomed to ride the streetcars free when they were wearing their little black bonnets. One Sunburst leader replied, perhaps recalling the reputation of the Berkeley streets, that *they* should wear crash helmets!

Wisdom comes often from "comic strips." In one of them not long ago the truth that "no man is an island unto himself" was reiterated. To which a youthful wise man in that strip retorted that such might be the truth but some persons were certainly "long, skinny peninsulas." There are a large number of persons incorporated into the strong, healthy, central body of the church by very tenuous connections— skinny peninsulas connected only by nostalgia or guilt or by one or two personal relationships. We hope Sunburst will greatly reduce the number of long, skinny peninsulas in our parish.

There were few such peninsular persons in the church of the New Testament. Many an American Protestant is considerably shaken by the report of Christian communism in the book of Acts where "all who believed were together and had all things in common; and they sold their possessions and goods and distributed them to all, as any had need." But sometimes we are so disturbed by the thought of that gigantic and irreversible garage sale that we fail to note that the emphasis is not on the sale but on everyone using everything he possesses to meet the needs of others within the fellowship. There will be things more difficult to surrender than our property if everyone is to help everyone else to a higher level of self-esteem. But that is one step on the road to the rest of that text, for the little flock where people are so loved, now as then, will be possessed by "glad and generous hearts" and have as a consequence a special gift for "praising God and having favor with the people."

·II·

Where the Rules
Are Flexible

After fourteen committees had studied the question and made in-
conclusive reports, after three and one half years of research and four
nine-page questionnaires, after three all-day church meetings and
twenty-seven sermons devoted to various aspects of the problem and
2,892 personal conversations, the little flock in my care voted by a
majority of three to change the hour of Sunday morning worship from
eleven o'clock to ten o'clock. Then the storm broke loose, "the rains
came down, the floods rose, the wind blew and beat upon that house"
of God, but somehow by the working of divine grace it stood. It was
thus proved beyond the possibility of contradiction that the rule by
which we had lived for ninety-three years, namely that 11:00 A.M.
Sunday is the divinely ordained time for public worship, was not, after
all, inflexibly established for all eternity. Of course, it is true that
some people have never adjusted to the change, and one lady continues
her own little private protest movement. Nonetheless a change was
made in one of the rules by which we live. Indeed, at this writing, a
further change in this rule is being darkly whispered in our churchly
cloisters.

When Virginia Satir summarized the qualities she had observed in
vital and nurturing families she included the notation that these families appear to live by "rules that are flexible, human, appropriate and
subject to change." My word! That comes as a real threat to all of us

sturdy, traditional types who have long maintained that the times and places and ordering of worship, the arrangement for the offering, the tune of the Doxology, and the location of the organ pipes must remain unchanged for the single and clear reason that "we have always done it that way." Those are the rules of the game. We have not really inquired if they are "human" or "appropriate," but we certainly do know that they are not "flexible" or "subject to change."

Such gentle sarcasm about the difficulty in making changes in public worship will sound terribly dated to scores of American Protestants. About the only certainty in many churches in recent years has been change itself. Recently the stereotype of public worship has changed from organ pipes and "Sunday best" to balloons and guitars and blue jeans. These changes have been backed up by highest authority and that authority has been widely quoted, "The Sabbath was made for man" (surely He would have said "persons,"), not persons "for the Sabbath!" Jesus' scorn for the development of minute and rigid details for the observance of the Sabbath arose when those rules became ends in themselves and no longer served the glory of God or the good of mankind. The fathers of Israel in pressing the importance of the letter of the rule rather than its good purpose goaded Jesus to deep resentment and he protested.

In the epistle to the Ephesians with its warm pastoral accent which reinforces the themes of these chapters we find this remarkable admonition to part of that early congregation: "Fathers, don't goad your children to resentment." The little flock needs guidance and rules, but when those rules become sanctified and rigid and ends in themselves they goad to resentment the children they were originally designed to help.

Yet all human communities need rules. We get into trouble when we forget that original sin is forever marked in our society, as P. T. Forsyth reminded us, by our cash registers and our elaborate systems for checking up on one another. So rules are made for the good of the family but they need constant and open review. Are they flexible? Are they human? Are they appropriate? Are they subject to change? Every parish church needs to review its rules in light of these questions.

However, it is crucial to note that the family counselor in appraising vital and nurturing families discovered *flexible* rules, not the *absence* of rules. The alternative community which we considered in the introduction offered a "community," so they said in their advertisement, "with no human restrictions or qualifications except for our common humanity." But later on in the prospectus reality emerged when in the final paragraph that alternative community is described as an "alternative *structure*." Now a structure has some sort of "human restrictions," a framework to hold it together and to give it being, or else it collapses like a house of sand with the first rivulet to wash against it. Our plea for the local church is for flexibility in the structure, not for the elimination of the framework.

Take, for example, creeds or statements of faith. I was reared in a congregation which recited the Apostles' Creed every Sunday and I know it by heart. I do not believe there has been a time in my life when I would have repudiated every phrase in it nor has there been a time when I could personally affirm every phrase in it. Fortunately, neither that creed nor the more contemporary and graceful Statement of Faith of the United Church of Christ has ever been proposed in the community of my heart as a "test of faith." Both are offered as a structure or framework reflecting the wisdom and experience of other persons in other periods of human history within which I could explore and question and grow in a present community of faith. Those statements are flexible, but in their broad affirmation, they are not expendable. Like the United States Constitution they are "both an instrument of power and a symbol of restraint." They are monotheistic; they are Christocentric; they affirm the corporate nature of Christian faith. When these rules remain flexible in application they are magnificently *inclusive;* when they become rigidly dogmatic and inflexible, they are *exclusive* and in the light of Jesus Christ must be judged inappropriate to the community of which he is the head. But he *is* the head. The little flock has *that* restriction and *that* qualification or it is not an instance of the Christian church.

From time to time those outward and acknowledged rules have spawned, for good or ill, some inward and unacknowledged rules which affect the whole atmosphere of the local church in our time quite as much as the acknowledged doctrinal structure. For many

Protestants, descended from Luther or Calvin or Wesley or Edwards, there remain some assumed rules, maintained with varying degrees of conviction and inflexibility, about conduct and human relationships which badly need some new flexibility if the local church is to have new heart and new being.

Consider, for example, some unexpressed rules about "anger." If someone "blows his stack," as we say, in a church committee meeting, everyone is embarrassed and fears that the whole enterprise is "down the tube" and good relationships forever shattered. An unspoken rule about good Christians keeping their tempers has been broken and everyone busily and pathetically squirms and tries to arrange a great "cover-up."

It is good, of course, to have some guidelines about anger. Anger is a very strong emotion and it can rock the little flock and knock it a deadly blow if it is not handled wisely. But, like the Jews in Jesus' time and the rule about the Sabbath, we have misunderstood the assumed rule about anger and have thought that it was an inflexible "no, no." "A Christian doesn't get angry with other Christians," we have supposed. "If he can't be sweet, he must be silent." Whenever some people hear of a good church row, they shake their heads and cluck their tongues and assume that this proves that those people are a bunch of hypocrites. "Christians love each other," it is said. "How could they possibly get angry with one another?"

Sometimes it is observed that people don't have such fights at the theater or symphony concert or even in restaurants where there are people assembled, doing something together in a group. Of course, the difference is in the depth of the relationship and in the "heart-felt" meaning of coming together. If people have their worst quarrels at home and at church, it may be because they quarrel the hardest over things which mean the most to them or where they really interact in a vital way with other persons. A family counselor once said, "Show me a family that does not quarrel and I will show you a family that will fall apart."

The rule about anger has been overdone and misunderstood if it rules anger out, tries to prohibit it or to hide it. Reinhold Niebuhr's famous sermon on "Anger and Forgiveness" finds its text in this same part of Ephesians: *"If* you are angry" (the italics are mine)—not *"Don't* be angry,"* or "Don't let your anger show," but *"if* you are angry, do not let anger lead you into sin; do not let sunset find you still nursing it."

In the church there must be room for the appropriate expression of anger, but it must not be allowed to cause permanent alienation or to corrode into hatred or into that egoistic corruption of anger which ensues when one deliberately nurses it and makes it a way of life. Some members of particular congregations (and churches) who have been rightly angry about the misuse of alcohol have made that anger into a way of life and tried to make Prohibition the inflexible rule of the whole church for all its members, discounting other ways of handling that problem. Other members in other times who have been rightly angry over war have made that anger into a way of life and tried to make pacifism the inflexible rule of the whole church for all its members, discounting other ways of spiritual growth and working for peace. There is a self-righteousness in the permanently angry person or permanently angry church which is a faithless and egoistic corruption of anger that is God-given energy to oppose evil.

In *To God Be the Glory* Ernest Campbell of the Riverside Church in New York City writes, "I need protection against the fanaticism of the *one-cause* man. He is legion in our society, moving everywhere with white-heat passion, reducing history to a single issue and a single solution, the one he happens to be pushing." [1] That kind of self-righteousness, the permanently "angry young man," has crippled many a local church in recent years, operating under the supposition that anger at social injustice can only be expressed in absolutist terms and exclusive programming. The orthodoxies of some liberal activists are quite as rigid and suffocating as the orthodoxies of the conservative fundamentalists. For example, if you are stirred by injustice in agricultural labor, the orthodoxy is to support even secondary boycotts, ignoring their negative influence on minority employment in urban areas. Such orthodoxies in some church circles are treated as divinely ordained and to question them is heresy.

1. Quoted in *Bulletin of the Congregational Library,* vol. 25, no. 2 (Winter 1974).

The biblical claim that all human beings are finite creatures often appears to apply to everyone but us and ours. I suspect that sort of spiritual deficiency in the left wing of the modern church may lie behind the contention of a minister friend who is more conservative than I. He argued with me one day that evangelicals in the American church scene differ from liberals, as he views us in my church, not only theologically and politically, but also in their capacity to laugh at themselves. When he underscored his claim by showing me a magazine published by evangelicals which lampooned Billy Graham, I was surprised and impressed. In a take-off on baseball trading cards promoted by bubble-gum manufacturers, the editors of *The Wittenburg Door* [2] prepared a series of religious trading cards. The back of each picture carried brief biographical material. On Billy Graham's, under the rubric of "Career Highlights," it read: "As boy practiced preaching in field near home. Converted two rabbits and three mules who have since become pastors of independent Baptist churches." When *The Christian Century* or *Christianity and Crisis* makes room in their columns for religious trading cards featuring their religious-political heroes (not their enemies), I will moderate this friendly observation about humor and faith in the left wing of the American church.

Exaggerated or not, such an observation may incline us to reflect on the deeper truth behind the words of Julian Hartt, "I lament a world," he writes, "that makes preachers of clowns rather than clowns of preachers. I lament a world that insists on making laughter self-accusation and every tear a reflex of guilt." [3] Every little flock may well pray for the gift of spontaneous human laughter which brings perspective to the minister's pretensions and the choirmaster's foibles and provides joyous evidence that the little flock really does have "heart."

There are other unacknowledged rules in many mainline congregations which need more flexibility in order to be human and appropriate for a community which owns Christ as Lord. Consider, for example, the outward expression of affection. Much the same can be said about it as has been said about anger. We have been taught not to

---

2. Published in San Diego by Youth Specialties.
3. Julian Hartt, *The Restless Quest* (Philadelphia: United Church Press, 1975).

display our feelings. Nice people keep such things to themselves and act as though they loved everybody the same and that not much.

I have been a minister in the same congregation—descendents of New England Yankees and midwestern pilgrims—for the better part of two decades. There have been many changes in that time but the one which surprises me the most is the spectacular increase in that congregation of general hugging and kissing! Some of us are never going to get our own internal rules flexed up enough to participate fully in that new atmosphere, but sometimes we get caught up in it without warning.

Again, in this instance, our fathers passed along a rule against too much familiarity to guard against sexual promiscuity. That rule soon was frozen into an inflexible absolute of no outward physical expression of caring between persons except one's declared single love and members of one's immediate family.

My father and mother enjoyed the close friendship of another couple all their adult years but never once did I hear the women addressed by the men or even by each other using their first names. I cannot imagine any outward physical expression of affection between those couples beyond a handclasp even in the midst of the griefs and sorrows which they ultimately came to share. Their behavior upon my father's death differed dramatically from that of a next-door neighbor, an old-country Italian, known only over the garden fence with a few vegetables or flowers passed back and forth and family comings and goings the subject of friendly conversation. When word of my father's death reached her ears, she came at once to the front door and into the house and headed straight across the room toward my defenseless mother and enveloped her in arms and tears. My mother, so touched by this honest and spontaneous and outward physical expression of sympathy, wept openly and refreshingly for the first time. So the fathers, making inflexible rules out of common cautions regarding the expression of anger and affection, have goaded another generation into resentment. And now times are changing.

Like all changes, thoughtful care needs to be exercised. Throughout this book there are repeated pleas for openness—in the first chapter, openness to one another in helping to confer new being: self-esteem.

In the chapter following this one, openness is urged to one another in communication, revealing and recreating truth. In this chapter openness is urged in the structure which holds our common life together, flexibility in the rules. Yet a caution needs expression; containers open at both ends are soon empty. The same may be true of communities of faith.

T. S. Matthews claims that Irving Babbitt was the professor who influenced T. S. Eliot most in his undergraduate days at Harvard. Eliot remembered Babbitt saying, "It is well to open one's mind, but only as a preliminary to closing it, only as a preparation, in short for the supreme act of judgment and selection." Well, that supreme act must be performed if we are to fulfill our humanity—and that act is a supremely religious act. It is necessary for the local church as well as the individual. It is a matter of value and faith, of loyalty and commitment.

Yes, indeed, times are changing, but that change may be disastrous if it is based on the idea that communities of love and faith can live without rules altogether any more than the secular community can. There is evidence that in some places rules which have evolved out of the wisdom of many generations are not being made more flexible and more human and more appropriate, but are being cast aside altogether. In *The Angle of Repose,* a novel about the writing of a historical novel, Wallace Stegner utilizes selected facts from the actual lives of an earlier generation.[4] The novel moves back and forth between the last century and the present time in which the writer, portraying himself as a man in his late fifties, often pauses to reflect on the contrast between the values of his grandparents whose history he is writing and those of his liberated son and his son's generation.

In one scene of such reflection a young woman, Shelley Rasmussen, his secretarial aide, who in Berkeley has embraced the sexual mores of the new liberated youthful generation of the late 1960s protests the "inhibited" way he, as author, handles the sex scenes of his grandparents.

I know all that business about never seeing your wife naked. They were so puritan about their bodies in those days, it was bound to have screwed

4. Garden City, N.Y.: Doubleday, 1971.

up their minds. . . . Can you leave out anything that basic and still have a valid book? Modern readers might find a study of the Victorian sex life interesting and funny.

The writer continues:

> I felt like asking her if contemporary sexual attitudes are so much healthier than Grandmother's, how Grandmother managed to get through a marriage that lasted more than sixty years, while Shelley Rasmussen hides out in her parents' house at the age of twenty or so to escape the attentions of her liberated and natural lover. But I only said, "Interesting in what way? Funny, how?"

So the much heralded generation gap describes a troublesome reality in the local church. Margaret Mead is not very optimistic about our ability to manage it constructively. "At this breaking point," she writes, "between two radically different and closely related groups, both are inevitably very lonely, as we face each other knowing that they will never experience what we have experienced and that we can never experience what they have experienced. . . ."

But the gospel suggests that such alienation need not persist. Perhaps the little flock provides one of the few meeting places across such gaps. Insofar as it does, it, as well as all the Shelley Rasmussens of our culture, may well ponder Rollo May's words:

> A common practice in our day is to avoid working up the courage required for authentic intimacy by shifting the issue to the body, making it a matter of simple physical courage. It is easier in our society to be naked physically than to be naked psychologically or spiritually—easier to share our body than to share our fantasies, hopes, fears, and aspirations, which are felt to be more personal and the sharing of which is experienced as making us more vulnerable. For curious reasons we are shy about sharing the things that matter most. Hence people short-circuit the more "dangerous" building of a relationship by leaping immediately into bed. After all, the body is an object and can be treated mechanically.[5]

Many congregations are immeasurably impoverished by not being able to manage their differences and have been narrowed down into

5. Rollo May, *The Courage to Create* (New York: W. W. Norton & Co., 1975), p. 18.

their alienations. Those favoring the old rules are put on the defensive and, thus, cling all the more ardently to their position. The "no rules" division, goaded by much that is anachronistic in social mores, clings to its more permissive ideas with the enthusiasm of new converts and neither group possesses the spiritual energy and objective stance required to inquire seriously about its own position, its own rules. "Are they flexible, human, appropriate and subject to change?" Is there a way out of this impasse? Or must every congregation be narrowed down to like-minded persons and to those with cultural and political affinity, and so miss the richness of a broader membership? What is there—or more! *who* is there, in Carlyle Marney's words, "to correct the images of ourselves"?

The substance of the answer to that question in the community of Christian faith is suggested by a bumper strip which has made common a crucial truth: "Families that pray together stay together." That slogan as slogan gives offense—it is somehow tarnished and obscured. Prayer recommended as remedy corrupts its motivation, but there is a significant clue here to be heard.

Some of us may hear it better from a free-wheeling spirit like the late Alan Watts who was quick to castigate Christians "so self-consciously preoccupied with the things they ought and ought not to have done . . . that they are absorbed in themselves instead of in God." Years ago when he was chaplain at Northwestern University he wrote about the worship of the church, its prayers and services. Listen to his comments with the ear of one who is searching for that one rule, that one inflexibility, which, maintained, will provide creative breathing space for wide differences and encourage constructive energy to flow from them within the little flock. He wrote:

Liturgy [is a] corporate forgetting of human personalities in the adoration of God. . . .

The liturgy is corporate because everyday life is corporate; we do not live, we cannot exist as separate and isolated individuals. . . .

The liturgy is the concrete bond of union between Christians at every stage . . . of growth—the naive, the adolescent and the mature. . . .

All can find common ground at the symbolic level, provided [they are not all expected, at all stages,] to understand it in the same way.[6]

So it may well be that to pray together *is* to stay together. We began our consideration of flexible rules for the little flock with some gentle teasing about the momentous difficulty which the congregation encounters when it attempts to change the time or style of public worship. There is always tremendous resistance and it has long been supposed that this is due to the fact that we are creatures of habit and that the change of a long-established schedule is very dislocating to almost everyone involved. All of which is undoubtedly true.

Yet I am wondering if there is another and deeper source of resistance to change in public worship.[7] Is that resistance the disguised and sometimes distorted but nonetheless crucial exercise of the survival instinct of the church? Does the little flock somehow intuitively *know* that the one rule which cannot be broken or changed if the flock is to live is the rule requiring it to meet regularly, in season and out, and to meet in the name of Christ? "Where two or three are gathered in my Name," that is the essence, the irreducible minimum of corporate worship, and it is the irreducible definition of every particular little flock which is identified as the church of Jesus Christ.

"For all their waywardness," writes Douglas John Hall in *The Reality of the Gospel and the Unreality of the Churches,* "and in spite of their capitivation by modernity, the churches still live with the tradition of Jerusalem; above all, they live with the Scriptures of the Jews and the early Christians. They have this link with the past. . . ."[8] To which I would add, ". . . and this link with the only future there is."

In recent years we have seen many new and so-called radical churches come into being—house churches, free churches, underground and above ground. But many of them were not truly radical

6. Alan Watts, *Behold the Spirit,* First Vintage Book Edition (New York: Random House, 1972), p. 236.
7. For another or supplementary interpretation of resistance in the congregation, see James Dittes, *The Church in the Way* (New York: Charles Scribner's Sons, 1967).
8. Douglas John Hall, *The Reality of the Gospel and the Unreality of the Churches* (Philadelphia: Westminster Press, 1975), p. 173.

in the sense of getting to the root of what it is to be the church. They were like that estimable journal, *Radical Religion,* published in Berkeley, California, which would be more accurately identified if it were called *The Religion of Radicals.* The "radical" churches were widely involved in many causes for justice and peace, but when they came to neglect their regular meeting together in Christ's name, the reading of the Scripture, the breaking of bread, the recital of God's saving story, the liturgy of salvation history, they began to die. Without this vertical and transcendental dimension to their life, such communities could not handle for long the tensions of their horizontal relationships. The church of Jesus Christ lives and grows as it meets to acknowledge that Jesus is Lord. It has that restriction and qualification over its "common humanity."

Can it be that if an ordinary congregation, encouraged by a more flexible generation coming along, finds rules to live by which make it permissible for its members to be more in touch with their feelings of anger and affection, it may also discover new freedom for them to be in touch with their feelings about God and to express them in worship and prayer? May it discover again the spiritual wisdom expressed by an unknown English country parson living and writing from the East Midlands of Great Britain probably during the latter half of the fourteenth century, who reminded his people that it is love, not knowledge, but love which "may reach up to God Himself even in this life?" [9]

So it may be that in the last quarter of the twentieth century we may be set free from the presumptions and perils of the Age of Reason and its proud descendants, set free by our children who have been "goaded into resentment," set free to be in touch with our feelings, and set free to celebrate God's love anew in corporate worship. Then the common liturgy and the common prayer will have meaning again; worship will not be an isolated and generational act but a mode of life for every little flock, glorifying God and enjoying him forever, binding a diverse family together in creative unity and taking heart.

9. *The Cloud of Unknowing,* tr. by Clifton Wolters (New York: Penguin Books, 1968), p. 65.

Helpful suggestions about rules for the local congregation arise in that queen of the epistles, the Ephesians, because while that epistle is *implicit* about flexibility, "Fathers, don't goad your children to resentment," it is first *explicit* about the worship of him in whom the whole structure of the church, surely including its proper rules, "is bonded together and grows into a holy temple in the Lord" (Ephesians 2:22).

·III·

Where the Truth
Is Spoken

In sketching the story of the Sunday school movement, Robert Lynn and Elliott Wright picture for us the missionaries of the Sunday School Union making their way from village to village across Pennsylvania, Ohio, and Indiana a century ago. Under the strict rules of the Union these earnest persons made their way on foot. Instructions from the Philadelphia office ruling out the use of horses actually read, in part: ". . . a horse tempts one to go too fast. Besides the missionary is generally welcome because he can talk as well as eat. His horse is unwelcome because he eats but cannot talk." [1]

So from the earliest day "talk" has been welcomed by lonely and isolated people but even more, human speech has been crucial and creative in gospel and church. It is interesting to learn that Virginia Satir also discovered good communication to be a common characteristic in vital and nurturing families. If we are concerned to help transform a local church into a vital and nurturing community, we may well reflect on the discovery that in those natural families best equipped to develop the potential of their members "communication is direct, clear, specific and honest." [2]

In that little flock in Ephesus where self-esteem was encouraged and

1. *Big Little School* (New York: Harper & Row, 1971), p. 27.
2. Virginia Satir, *Peoplemaking* (Palo Alto, Ca.: Science & Behavior Books, 1972), p. 4.

flexibility in the rules was counseled, there was also the urging to "speak the truth to each other, for all of us are the parts of one body" (Ephesians 4:25, NEB). A family, whether of the flesh or of the heart, is a corporate entity like the human body. Its communication scheme by which it is linked into a whole is like the nervous system of the body. "A body can only function accurately and healthily," William Barclay reminds us, "when each part of it passes true messages to the brain and to the other parts." When false messages or no messages are sent, the body is in trouble.

One part of the body cannot be helpful or protective to another part or to the whole if it receives no messages or cannot trust the messages it does receive. Persons grow profoundly sick, neurotically or physically, when they get all kinds of wrong messages or learn by bitter experience that they cannot trust the ones they receive. If pain comes through as pleasure and good is sensed as evil, the body and the spirit are in trouble, energy is wasted in huge amounts, and danger, genuine and real, stalks every path those persons walk and threatens every good they undertake.

Is this not the affliction summarized under such titles as Teapot Dome or Watergate which tears at the health and function of our nation? When yesterday's "damnable lies" are today's excruciating truths, the nervous system is sending untrustworthy messages and the whole body is palsied with involuntary tremors, energy is wasted and danger threatens, because that family cannot trust the messages it receives. When truth is cut into half-truths, the nation's effectiveness is also cut in half or less, and its desperately needed reliability to lead in many a good thing—like justice at home and peace abroad—is grievously, if not totally, compromised. When half-truths and whole lies clog the nervous system of a nation or a family, that body grows profoundly sick. So "speak the truth to each other, for all of us are the parts of one body."

So with the local congregation, the truth must be spoken for the same compelling reasons. How many local churches have their nervous systems clogged with poor communication, not necessarily self-serving lies, but thoughtless assumptions or careless indifference to the feelings and efforts of others? Satir tells of a "young man whose mother was accusing him of violating an agreement to tell her when he was going out. He insisted that he *had* told her. As evidence he said, 'You saw me ironing a shirt that day, and you know I never iron a shirt for myself unless I am going out!' "

Poor communication makes it hard for any parish church to thrive in the matters which really count, such as exercising "love like Christ's" and building up self-esteem among its members, let alone sustaining an Amos or hearing this world's Rachels. It is difficult for a parish to thrive at this level without excellent communication because it lives not only on trust but on making clear the caring which is its common bond and life secret. It is better to have gigantic quarrels—or even little ones—than superimposed peace, because then there is at least direct communication. That is far better than to suppose that "silence is golden" and to imagine that all is lovely because nothing disquieting is ever expressed.

However, Christian persons have a religious responsibility to be aware of the difference between that which is "disquieting or controversial" and that which is ugly, hurtful, or mean in spirit. That early parish in Ephesus was urged, as we have said, to "speak the truth to each other," but it was also urged not to allow bad language among its members but only to speak what "is good and helpful to the occasion." There is often a greater burden of idle, thoughtless talk in parish churches than any other institution could suffer and still endure. That is no reason to countenance it, but rather, to view it as the symptom that it is. It will be quieted not by preachments but by discovery of the hidden needs which such idle talk may reveal and the low self-esteem it may shroud.

There was something instinctively right and wise about the God-fearing mother, the wife of a Methodist bishop, who lived on our block when I was a child. I was terrified by the news circulated in the junior circles of that neighborhood to the effect that she washed out her son's mouth with soap when he used foul words. I suspected she would feel free to do the same to me! At least I would have had a personal encounter at a similar level with her husband, the bishop! A free-wheeling permissive generation of parents bent on free expression shudder at the thought of such a soaping and at that old-fashioned imposition of authority and standards. A trusted colleague protested this illustration. He has discovered growth and liberation in groups where carefulness of speech is abandoned in favor of freedom of expression, but I do not believe such freedom is the final word. In the long run, truth and goodness may need that mother's emphasis, for whenever we debase our speech, we debase our humanity. Speech is a rare and precious gift, much underestimated by many specialists in communication who view it primarily as an instrument to convey ideas or information. Faith knows that it is much more, as we shall consider in Chapter IV. Enough for now to acknowledge that language is a great and holy mystery and that words are symbols and symbols participate in the reality they symbolize. Or why the sacraments? Or the shock of profanity?

So that fast-moving mother with her bar of soap underscored the truth which philosophers and theologians try to explain and my colleague in encounter groups had overlooked while "experiencing." Father Ong in *Presence of the Word* makes it clear that because of the very nature of sound and its capacity to search out the interior, "voice has a kind of primacy in the formation of the communities of men." And that communication is not simply a way of "contacting" one another, as some persons careless in grammar and casual in theology say, but the "means of entering into the life and consciousness of others." [3]

Yet a mother may do more harm than good if the primary message she conveys is that foul language is primarily dirty words. The child becomes an adolescent and repudiates the teaching about obscene language because he hears the power of clean and proper words used by clean and proper parents to destroy other people, not simply to describe evil but to empower it and bring it to expression. This sin is not left only to politicians and commentators on the public scene. Have we not heard it often shuddering the very framework of the little flock?

Bad language can be no spoken words at all, of course. It can be body language or worse, the menace of the unspoken word. Eugene

3. Walter J. Ong, *Presence of the Word* (New York: Simon & Schuster, 1970), pp. 15, 124.

Kennedy, a Catholic priest, puts it in his book, *The Pain of Being Human,* when he describes that silent person who "knows just when to withhold support, just when not to answer a letter or when to drop out so that the maximum effect is achieved. He can look all innocent and say, 'I never did anything,' but in reality [he has let] his own hostility seep out slowly to poison the stream of life all around him." [4]

The silent critic, the silent dropout, is one of the most pernicious problems in the local church. A recent book by John Westerhoff III, *Values For Tomorrow's Children,* calling for a radical change in Christian education is almost spoiled for me by the casual way he reports on church dropouts as though that were the only decent way for disgruntled or disappointed people to handle their disillusionment with the church. Sometimes I feel Westerhoff himself unwittingly uses "dropping out" as an indirect threat to every churchgoing Christian who reads the book. If your church is not a place of acceptance like Paul Tillich's living room, he seems to say, that promising seminary student will "leave the church"; if the official board doesn't agree to the young people's suggestion about a fair-housing pledge, a number of the young people will leave the church "at least for the time and, perhaps, forever." Westerhoff agrees with Ellis Nelson "that faith is communicated by a community of believers and that the meaning of faith is developed by its members out of their history, by their interaction with each other, and in relation to the events that take place in their lives." [5] I also agree. Therefore, to "drop out" of that community comes very close to being the sin against the Holy Spirit. My heroes are those like Westerhoff himself who, deeply discouraged, stay in the community and urge clearer and clarifying communication, of which his book on Christian education is an instance.

"Speak the truth. . . ." The local church needs to give constant attention to the channels of communication, for they require daily tending. There is little promise in that parish which can only communicate pleasant and affable messages, which can discover truth only if it is

4. Eugene C. Kennedy, *The Pain of Being Human* (New York: Doubleday, 1974), p. 25.
5. John H. Westerhoff, *Values for Tomorrow's Children* (Philadelphia: Pilgrim Press, 1971), p. 9.

easy to receive. We need the presence of what Paul, a blind writer in
one of Elizabeth Goudge's novels, found in the heroine: "He . . .
found in her what he had never had—a sympathetic but intelligent
critic. She could wield the pruning knife mercilessly yet at the same
time she watered the roots." That is a fine art and much appreciated,
although I must confess that sometimes my suspicions are raised so
high when someone overwaters my roots that I wish he would hurry
up and get the pruning over with! But in the instance of the contemporary local church I believe it is time to let the pruning go awhile
and tend to watering the roots!

There is a rule for all such communication in the parish church. It
follows Father Ong's conviction about the particular nature of sound
possessing a communicative power quite lacking in visual communication. Vision of itself tends to depersonalize relationships. How
better to unhinge another than to stare at him? Without speech or a
substitute, staring reduces us to a "non-person," an object. Ong puts
it: "Speech establishes the specifically human relation that takes the
edge off the cruelty of vision." So the rule is this: seek direct spoken
communication whenever possible and do not expect the written word
to serve as an adequate substitute. Many local churches, as they grow
larger, feel that they must abandon the monthly church meeting or its
equivalent and substitute the newsletter. What a pity. Yet they do so
because the church meeting has been no "meeting." It has become a
place for reports to be made, a place much too large for conversation
and often dominated by one or two or the same half-dozen particularly
verbal persons in any church, including the minister.

Fortunately we live in a time when new attention has been brought
to bear on groups and how they operate. The alternative to the dull or
dominated church meeting is not to give up the spoken word and rely
upon the written word. There are countless other ways to plan and
conduct a meeting which give everyone a chance to speak and be
heard. In terms of "loving like Christ" and building up self-esteem, it
is absolutely essential to the little flock that such opportunities for ver-
balization are provided. It has been well said that most people don't
mind being voted down, but they heartily resent not being heard.

Some years ago our congregation was confronted with some basic and costly decision-making following a disastrous fire which destroyed our place of worship just at the time we were trying to devote more of our resources of people and money to the urban-racial crisis. The leadership of the church moved speedily after the fire. Before there was time for divergent opinions to crystallize and harden into fervently held dogma with a lot of ego commitment to each particular point of view, a church meeting was called "to reason together" about our situation. Several hundred people came and after a short statement of the situation and the reason for the special meeting, the moderator, much to everyone's surprise, divided us into groups of seven or nine persons and sent us to separate locations tucked in corners of all the remaining rooms and halls of the church buildings. Each group was to choose a discussion leader and a recorder. We were instructed to discuss our ideas about what we should do and list the dominant concerns of each group. After ninety minutes, we reassembled and every different idea was listed on endless sheets of butcher paper around the walls. Although it sounds as though we were dealing with hundreds of items, actually many were practically duplicates and as the evening progressed the list shook down into a few dozen primary concerns plus a number of carefully noted peripheral or idiosyncratic suggestions. Those lists stayed up for many months until a plan of action was worked out by a democratically elected committee and submitted for discussion. The first report of that committee included every idea on the wall, and explained either *where it was* specifically incorporated into the proposal or *why it was not.* Discussion ensued, and in almost every instance there was consensus. Where there was not, further discussion and meetings provided ample opportunity to present opposing points of view and then finally to take a vote. All this is cited as only one very simple way by which even large parishes can rely upon verbal communication. Using a similar format, we have found it possible to have excellent conversation and get appropriate direction about such issues as amnesty and criminal justice. Much careful planning is required and both biblical and contemporary input must be included.

Cassette tapes are a tremendous help in implementing the conviction that the spoken word is much to be preferred, ordinarily, to the written word. John Goodlad, dean of the Graduate School of Education at UCLA, is on fire about the need for change in American public education. He has published almost a dozen books and numerous written studies. Now he has taken to the tape, the "talking book." Goodlad and his producers recognize the limitations of tapes but list some of the overriding advantages, "namely, the personality and emotions of the speaker could animate the content and give new life to what otherwise might be considered an overworked topic." [6] Those who do not want the true meaning of the White House conversations revealed do well to keep the tapes written to be read and not oral to be heard.

The imagination is stimulated by the possibilities that the inexpensive cassette offers the church, which is essentially and correctly an oral institution. Bible or Lenten groups organized in neighborhoods can be sparked by a taped message from the minister tied into the text or lesson or theme for the following Sunday. The incapacitated members of the congregation in days past have been called "shut-ins." They were usually in actuality "shut-outs," save for occasional calls from church friends. Now many churches which could never justify the expense of a radio broadcast of their service can take the Sunday service or a recorded church meeting to the home-bound members. The little flock will find the tape a great gift in combating urban loneliness and the isolation of the sick. It also has tremendous possibilities in the outward mission of the local church, which we will consider in the final chapter.

Many ministers learn to dread the Every Member Canvass, the annual stewardship program, when callers reach into every home. The dread is not economic. It comes about because that calling always brings to the minister's attention every unhappy and disgruntled person in the parish. With us, however, all this changed dramatically after the Sunburst program described in Chapter I got under way. The Every Member Canvass uncovered almost no unhappy and disgruntled persons. Everyone already had had opportunity to talk with someone "from the church"; there was almost no one who could honestly say, "No one from the church ever calls upon me except when they want money." Indeed, that "they" syndrome has largely disappeared because communication has improved and fewer people feel on the outside.

6. *Saturday Review,* March 1973.

All of this about communication in the parish and especially about human speech is of more than passing interest because the church itself, as another has said, is a Speech Event. Her Lord appeared in the Word made flesh. At Pentecost, the Torah, the great things God had done, was spoken in every tongue. God's righteousnesses are re-created always into every future by speaking and telling and talking. The counsel to the church in Ephesus was not simply "to keep talking." It was not "speak to each other," although that might be a place for some congregations to begin if they wish to become vital and nurturing fellowships. No, the admonition to that early congregation was to "speak the truth to each other, for all of us are the parts of one body."

"Speak the *truth!*" What is that? It sounds like a package deal. Here is truth, all wrapped up in the Bible or the tradition or the liturgy or the latest "in vogue" theological treatise to be delivered by word of mouth. "Speak the truth." All that again overlooks the creative power of speech itself, of conversation. It does not understand that ideas do not appear full blown in the abstract and then are delivered by words. Rather, words and human speech itself are partners in the creation of ideas.

So when the little flock seeks to speak the truth, it is not some pronouncement to be made, but a *happening* to encourage. The prophetic church is not guaranteed by bold and brave resolutions but by a kind of life in itself and conversation with the world which helps expose the verities of a very great God. We do well to remember (as Heidegger reminds us) that the expression which the Greeks used to convey the notion of "truth" meant "unhiddenness." Truth is a discovery and the adventure which leads to it is the adventure of communication, human-human and thus human-divine. In a nurturing parish it is a discovery in which all the members are engaged. It is not propaganda handed down or forced upward. It is not nurtured by the attitude which says in effect or is expressed in fact as, "Now if you want the truth in a nutshell, here it is. Listen to me." A person who comes on that way in pulpit or pew, in church meeting or family conclave needs to be gently reminded that the only thing that really fits in a nutshell is a nut.

Preaching is one of the most widely misunderstood and abused gifts of the church. The "talk-back" method of increasing interest and participation in preaching and Christian worship demonstrates a concern for improving communications in the church. It provides an opportunity to be "direct, clear, specific and honest," but in the process seriously compromises the sacramental nature of the sermon. To engage in such a "talk-back" arrangement sometimes appears a little like adjourning to the church kitchen after Holy Communion to discuss the recipe for the bread. Christian preaching seeks to be a channel of God's address to the whole person, his body and feeling and intellect. The sermon "talk-back" arrangement is an overreaction to sermons which never reached the life of feeling. It is appropriate if sermons are lectures and their primary function is to educate, but if that is the limit of a sermon's function, we may well abandon it to more effective educational methods.

Many American ministers embrace such questionable methods in an altogether appropriate concern to increase the level of communication within and from the little flock. But in the process they sacrifice their integrity as theologians. It comes about also because of widespread ignorance about the Bible. They wrestle with the problem of presenting what Charles R. Brown used to call "the eternal truths of the Old Testament and of the New" to contemporary Americans whose interest in the Bible is at about the same level as their understanding of it, which comes nowhere near as high as that elephant's eye of a beautiful morning.

As an alternative to the "talk-back" after the sermon has been preached, our congregation has long had sermon seminars as part of the preparation of preacher and people before the sermon is preached. This method recognizes that the whole congregation is addressed by God's Holy Word and shares the responsibility with the minister to be a channel for the inestimable grace of God which may flow through the Word preached as well as the Bread broken. What is this method for which so much is so presumptuously claimed?

The basic design is simple and many creative variations are possible and desirable. In the usual one the preacher for the following Sunday meets with any members of the congregation who wish to come together to reflect on the passage of Scripture determined as the text for that Sunday. We have had many variations on this basic pattern. It has been important not to allow such meetings to get into a rut. Therefore, we have never held such seminars fifty-two weeks a year and we never continue a series of them in the same time and place for more than a few months, usually less. In this fashion the membership of the seminar shifts and it does not simply become the Wednesday Night Prayer Meeting in disguise with the same faithful saints year after year.

In a typical seminar the process is very simple and informal. The passage to be considered is announced on the preceding Sunday. One Lent we covered the seven major sections of Romans. That was pretty heavy fare. Such abstract and philosophical passages of the Bible are the most difficult for this method. It is good to begin with more colorful and concrete sections. One series dealt with important meals in the life of Jesus. The parables are excellent material, of course. The hero stories in the Old Testament are easier to handle than Romans, although they present some obvious problems. A congregation which follows a lectionary will have no problems at this point and will avoid the dangers of subjective selection of Scripture. The new Lectionary prepared by COCU, along with the supplementary material in *Proclamation*, [7] is excellent.

The group comes prepared to discuss the passage. The leader, usually the minister except where we have had several groups meeting simultaneously and lay persons have been enlisted as assistants, gives a brief exegesis of the passage. He or she should not take more than six or seven minutes at the most. The purpose is only to remove obstacles and to set interpretive ground rules. For example, the passage might be the book of Jonah. The minister briefly would make clear that the seminar is not gathered to *debate* the nature of this literature and so for the purposes of *this* seminar it will be assumed that it is not a literal record of a personal experience. This is not so easily done with some other passages, but the preacher can afford to be arbitrary about such matters because the sermon to be prepared will be his responsibility.

Then the discussion begins. His goal is to discover an emerging

7. *Proclamation* is a series of brief commentaries based upon a three-year liturgical cycle. Published by Fortress Press, Philadelphia.

theme and cluster around it the existential reality of that congregation and the contemporary scene. The members are asked to be spontaneous and not hinder the movement of the Spirit by deciding that what comes to mind is trivial or unimportant. The minister may well frequently reassure the participants that the process of creativity demands giving attention to what presses to the surface of awareness. Concrete, specific material out of the life of feeling in the daily round is very helpful. The sermon is broadened by experience and reading far broader than any one person can possess. Recently a sermon included pertinent and clear illustrative material from William Blake and Lloyd C. Douglas, neither of whom is a current intimate of the preacher. Many artists and writers testify to the creativity of the process of free association. The leader may wish to bring the association back to the text from time to time, but he must not hinder it with his own presuppositions about how the text will shape the sermon. This can be a very exciting and productive process—not always, of course, but more often than some ministers find their own isolated reflections to be!

The usual skills of group process are important and the leader needs to keep strictly to his role as enabler of the discussion *and* as recorder. Unfortunately, some preachers will find it impossible to use a sermon seminar, much less lead one. The leader here is more the pastor than the preacher, sensitive to the person who needs room made so he can speak, and tactfully able to protect the overtalkative participant from his own anxiety. The leader-preacher listens carefully and makes brief notes about anything which strikes him or her as interesting and important. That is about all there is to it.

The seminar should end promptly at the agreed-upon time, usually not less than seventy-five minutes and not more than ninety. If it is a luncheon group of working persons, the time may have to be even less. The minister makes no commitment to use anything from the group in the coming sermon, but almost always the sermon is profoundly changed by the experience. Anonymity is preserved but the participating members know that the minister may use anything they contribute. No copyrights, no credits! In years of sermon seminars I have never had any complaint about material used or ignored. Recently a person complained jokingly that she didn't hear the sermon because she was listening for her contribution which, unfortunately, didn't come until the last three minutes. Once in a while the Sunday sermon bears little or no relationship to the seminar at all! But almost always the seminar proves to be a dominant influence.

Recently we have tried a very promising adaptation of this method. The congregation was invited to participate in preparing five sermons based on the Ten Commandments. There was to be a sermon seminar but with a twist! Instead of dividing the Ten Commandments some way and approaching them one by one (or two by two) and commencing each seminar with the brief exegesis, we announced that each seminar would deal with a "case study." The cases would be supplied in advance and then the seminar would help the preacher determine which one of the Ten Commandments was the most pertinent. There were a lot of surprises along the way. In only one instance did the obvious commandment prove to be the most pertinent one, as the case of Miss Harriet's Baby, included with its sermon in Appendix B, demonstrates.

We were fortunate in being able to draw on the skilled and gracious assistance of Dr. Keith R. Bridston who was interested in our particular approach to the case-study method, in which he has had wide experience.[8] His work has been largely in adapting the case-study method for theological education, but he helped us see its promise for the local parish. He suggested the first case, Wilson Distributors, which is a classical one, and he led the discussion of it to provide a model for subsequent sermon seminars in that series.

The second and third cases were prepared by members of the seminar, Professor Delmer Brown of the University of California, and the Reverend Kenneth Coates, now of Long Beach, California, then a member of our congregation. In each instance these persons led the discussion. In these case-study seminars the preacher participated very little. The first sermon in the series was delivered *before* the first seminar and established the ground rules and, incidentally, did much of

8. For a different use of the case-study method in the church, see *Casebook on Church and Society* (Nashville: Abingdon Press, 1974), of which Keith R. Bridston is one of the editors.

the exegesis for the entire series. In each seminar itself the minister took notes and listened to the conversation with great interest but usually spoke very little. However, if no specific commandment had been proposed and the seminar had only twenty or thirty minutes more to go, he spoke up and raised that question.

The fourth case study may have been a mistake. Certainly it presented some problems and not all related to sex! It was taken from a news account. There were not enough details. The leader, Ms. Annette Fuller, recognized this hazard and very wisely suggested that we manufacture some assumptions to narrow the problem. These are listed in the context of the case study (see Appendix B), but necessarily they introduced a measure of unreality into the discussion. When you do not know the details you are able to bypass or rationalize the knottier problems. However, this is the case study and sermon included in the appendix because of its relation to the life of feeling.

The realism and believability of the cases are exceedingly crucial. When they ring true to life they not only heighten interest and participation in the sermon and service, but they provide an objective place from which thorny issues may be considered without the preacher's known bias and other limitations getting in the way before the biblical witness is even considered.

Somewhere Marshall McLuhan criticizes education for being "programmed for instruction rather than for discovery." So it is too frequently with the church, not only in the preaching but in its total life. Parishes should be programmed for discovery. Then truth becomes "unhidden" in the everyday encounters in and with Scripture, tradition, and liturgy. They are all illumined or "unhidden" in experience and in mutual reflection on that experience in exciting conversation, "direct, clear, specific and honest." Such communication is always a two-way street with traffic kept flowing by empathy and smoothed out by the eagerness to hear. Truth is best experienced in that congregation where every member seeks the blessing Solomon asked: "Give thy servant a heart with skill to listen."

So the "network of caring," suggested in an earlier chapter, as well as the sermon seminars, relies upon this quality found in nurturing families, "communication which is direct, clear, specific and honest."

We need that to be reinforcing to one another as respeonsible members of the little flock. That may be in committee meeting or in private conversation or public encounter. In our parish, unaccustomed as we are to any public personal witnessing, we have recently found truth unhidden for us all by brief statements of personal experience offered as part of our Sunday worship. Here communication has been "direct, clear, specific and honest." The lay persons who have participated have done so with great sensitivity and reality and have provided much encouragement for us all.

A professor of aeronautical engineering who has found time to enjoy work with such different groups as the Boy Scouts and parolees from San Quentin Prison recently concluded such a witness with these words:

> This church is, in both direct and subtle ways, an ever-present comfort to me in times of personal professional crisis. Many of you may reasonably regard me as a callow youth, but I am old enough to sense that my intellectual aggressiveness isn't always what it used to be, and that there are many people on the faculty who are cleverer, wiser, or more energetic than I. Sometimes this realization is deeply depressing, particularly when I sense that I am letting down colleagues who thought that I would produce more than I have, and who have to look forward to 21 more years of me before I reach retirement age. Then something rescues me from this depression. It may be something tangible, like the loyalty and support of my beloved wife, or like the sense of trust and acceptance which I feel in this place. Perhaps it is divine grace, allowing me to feel that regardless of my worth, I am loved.
>
> And so, having known love; having witnessed courage, humility, compassion and dignity; I feel that I have truly lived. Somehow I am confident that when I die, no matter how rudely that event may interrupt my most cherished plans, life shall not have shortchanged me in any essential way. I know of no greater gift that any man may ask, and so I thank you, and with the prayer that you and I may be truly together in this moment, I thank God.

And with that communication—direct, clear, specific and honest—our congregation was truly together and with God. I hope you will agree with me that one does not have to say the word "Christ" like some magic formula in order to bear witness to him and to employ human speech to his unhiding.

·IV·

Where Hearing
Is Believing

Much that has been suggested in the last chapter and much that will be proposed in the next chapter rests upon the very important conviction that "hearing is believing." So we propose that the local church which wishes to increase in the grace and beauty of a vital and nurturing Christian community, a little flock of Christ, must incorporate into its understanding as well as into its experience the reality that "hearing is believing."

Many of us have accepted uncritically the opposite dictum, "seeing is believing." There is, however, a growing confidence in many disciplines that "hearing" is a far more extensive and profound experience than "seeing," primarily because of the preeminent and evocative role of human speech, or oral communication.

How far we have gone in the assumption of the priority of sight to sound is suggested by the common speculation among those who both see and hear adequately that, if they had to be deprived of either sight or hearing, they would choose to keep their sight. It may be presumptuous of one who is neither blind nor deaf to ruminate on such misfortune, but we all do. Most of the people I have asked fear blindness more than deafness. Many are surprised that there could be any question about it for anyone.

It might well be expected that the average person in our culture should reflect this feeling of the greater importance of sight because we have been a visual culture. The blind person is deprived of the visual symbols and to us as children of the "enlightenment" this "feels" like the primary deprivation a person could experience. Such a person must accommodate himself to very difficult and inadequate compensatory aids or else go without "reading, writing and arithmetic," which is to be cut off from the disciplines that have been the chief means for the development of civilization as we know it.

So Loren Eiseley, anthropologist and historian of science, writes in his beautiful rhythmic style about that epochal moment in mankind's long history when a way was invented

> to pass knowledge through the doorway of the tomb—namely, the achievement of the written word.
> Only so can knowledge be made sufficiently cumulative to challenge the stars.[1]

No one is disputing that! The written word has been the hand-maiden of external achievement. The stars have been challenged!

In similar fashion Walter J. Ong, the Jesuit scholar, reminds us of the absolute dependence of scientific development upon the visual symbol, the written sign and word. In his Terry Lectures of 1964, devoted to a brilliant exposition of the spoken word as man's primary medium of communication, he also made it perfectly clear that

> The large scale accumulation of exact knowledge which makes possible elaborate and dispassionate causal analyses and sharp abstract categorization depends absolutely on writing. Astronomy, math, physics, grammar, logic, metaphysics, remain mere potentials without it.[2]

An oral culture, as he reminds us elsewhere "does not produce a Descartes or Newton or Einstein." [3]

The Christian church has not lived apart from this visual culture. It has been aided by it and hindered by it. Is it not a curious grammatical validation of this theme that the corruption of the Scripture which has spoiled the Bible for countless persons of our time is called *literalism?* That means "following the letter." That perverse view of the

1. Loren Eiseley, *Invisible Pyramid* (New York: Charles Scribner's Sons, 1972), p. 63.
2. Walter J. Ong, *Presence of the Word* (New York: Simon & Schuster, 1970), p. 203.
3. Ibid., p. 232.

Bible seeks to endow the visual symbol, the written words and letters, with concocted divine authority. The tragic and devastating consequence is to bury in print the authority the Scripture does possess which is related to hearing and speech and divine address.

We sometimes hear people say, "If the Bible does not mean exactly what the words say . . . if it is not literally true, then it is not the word of God." Such irreverent and intemperate statements have been the source of incalculable mischief and harm. Such a demand which proposes "literal" truth as the only or ultimate truth makes one sad. It brings to mind Walter Ong's observations about the Chinese language where the writing system provides no letters upon which the concept *literal* can be built. The roughly equivalent concepts, he says, would be fairly translated into English as "according to the surface of the word," or "according to the dead character." Hardly laudatory expressions, he adds as a personal comment.[4] Demands for only the "literal" truth of the Bible or the literal truth of any of the language of faith, creed, hymns, prayers, dooms us to "surface" experiences and a "dead" religion.

Of course, the visual has played and should always continue to play an appropriate and positive place in the experience of the church. Every Protestant who explores the factors which contributed to the Reformation is soon introduced to the printing press. That instrument with its movable type was not an unmixed blessing but it was instrumental in the reform of the church. Long before that, visual symbols and written words were crucial to the awakening of faith—the fish scratched on the walls of the sewers of Rome as well as the letters of the Great Apostle. But the spiritual blockage of modern Christians begins in the intellectual and cultural assumption which forgets that Christianity was born in an oral culture and assumes that the visual is the most accurate and truthful of the sense perceptions.

So Christians with their religious faith dependent upon and rooted in and flowering out of oral experience have floundered in a visual culture. We have suffered intellectual embarrassment and religious poverty because our religion has not been truly "at home" in the objec-

4. Ibid., p. 47.

tified world of the visual. But perhaps a broader intellectual world is at hand, one that is open to the proposition that sound may be a more discerning and comprehensive experience than sight and which is prepared to understand that the spoken word is prior to the written word and has resources denied to visual symbols. Rabbi Abraham J. Heschel tried to turn us toward these long-neglected resources. "We shall never be able to understand that the spirit is revealed in the form of words," he wrote, "unless we discover the vital truth that speech has power. . . ." [5]

It is not my purpose to explore in detail the philosophical concepts which underlie the peculiar power that human speech, as a very crucial kind of sound, possesses. That is beyond my competence. My purpose is to share with you the excitement I have felt as a Protestant minister, as preacher and pastor and teacher and administrator, when I have touched down in the work of scholars in this field. It is the responsibility of "practitioners" in the church to respond to and help develop the life-giving work of those who have the talent and time to be professional philosophers and theologians.

A great breakthrough has already taken place in the "secular" world as this truth and its implications have been discovered. That world has already moved beyond the confines of a visual culture. The spoken word has new power among us as television replaces the newspaper, the transistor radio covers the face of the earth, and even the giant impersonal corporations have discovered that no round-robin office memo, however detailed and carefully written, can begin to match an airport conference for effectiveness. This breakthrough is not outside divine intent but part of the working of the Spirit. In it is a direct summons to the church to be up and about its task. The nature of that breakthrough is particularly significant to the church because it fairly shouts to Christians a directive about the potential power of the church's *own history* and *own experience* as an oral institution. When we are reminded that the church is a "speech event" the reference is not only to Pentecost or a Vatican Council but also to the little flock with its worship and committee meetings and retreats.

5. Quoted in Harold Stahmer, *Speak That I May See Thee!* (New York: Macmillan, 1968), p. 2.

The church will find there in its *own* genius as an oral institution the means by which it may move more adequately toward the goals set before it, the gospel goals, if you will, the eschatalogical realities which we call the Kingdom of God. This is not to urge a romantic return to medieval, pre-Gutenberg orality but to move beyond the typographical era into all the incredibly expanded universe, both personal and public, for individuals and the communities of mankind, which is close at hand. An oral institution which knows instinctively that "the letter kills, but the Spirit gives life" (II Corinthians 3:6), and has continued to honor the word *Word* with a far-spreading capital letter as though it were designed for flight through space and time on the waves of sound and into the soul of mankind, is ideally prepared for another Great Awakening in such an age, an age of sound.

This release of fresh power through the church will come about insofar as we are able to move beyond the limiting surface objectivity of sight, as we are able to move beyond the limited view of human experience which would propose as final truth that "seeing is believing," and move into the depths of man's spirit and God's Spirit which can be opened to us through the mystery of sound. Father Ong closed his Terry Lectures remembering that there is mystery in vision and in touch and in taste and in smell. "But the mystery of sound," he said, "is the most personally human, and in this sense closest to the Divine." [6]

Perhaps the parable for the church in this new age of sound is in the story of Paul's conversion. We have been taught the curious custom of speaking of that experience as Paul's *vision* on the road to Damascus. But it was his vision which was taken from him, lost in the scuffle with the Spirit, so he could be free to *hear* his Lord.

All of this mystery and power of sound and human speech may seem remote from the immediate and practical concern to help the local church become a vital and nurturing community, but it is also closely related to the life of feeling, to the gift of "Heart." Its importance will become clearer as we mention now two aspects of the mystery and power of human speech which bear with particular relevance upon the

6. Walter J. Ong, *Presence of the Word* (New York: Simon & Schuster, 1970), p. 324.

life of feeling and faith. The first one to consider will support the thesis in the preceding chapter about good communication and will clarify the rule proposed there about always preferring the spoken to the written word when working for good communication in the little flock. It also has profound implication for world mission, to be considered in the last chapter. Indeed, it touches the local church deeply at every point of its life. So note this first: *human speech may possess greater power than other forms of language to search out and reveal the interior of life, soul to soul, person to person, human and divine.*

In this quality to explore the interior of life, human speech may simply be the most personal and sensitive instrument of sound. We are familiar with this capacity of *sounding* in less highly developed tools. "Thus we tap a wall," Father Ong writes, "to discover where it is hollow inside, or we ring a silver-colored coin to discover whether it is perhaps lead inside. To discover such things by sight, we should have to open what we examine, making the inside an outside, destroying its interiority as such." [7] Ah, so rare a gift is the gift of speech, to explore and learn and share and reveal—soul to soul, person to person, human and divine.

Not long ago one of our sons wrote us a letter which we did not fully understand. It was disturbing, especially to my wife who is more intuitive in these matters than I. Finally I said to her, "Why don't you phone him? Once you hear his voice you will know how he really feels." That is a very common experience in our time. The spoken word promising clarity and intimacy is now more readily available and incredibly extended in effectiveness in this new age of sound.

Some members of the current youth cult have built up a big charge of hostility against the telephone company. They cite all the "sins" of American corporations to buttress their hostility. Some of them take delight in cheating Ma Bell and discovering new ways to bypass telephone charges. But even as they cheat the corporation they speak almost affectionately of Ma Bell and I wonder if their hostility is not in part the indignation unconsciously felt that any "impersonal corporation" should hinder with toll charges and coin boxes their "personal"

---

7. Walter J. Ong, *Presence of the Word* (New York: Simon & Schuster, 1970), p. 118.

relationships, their soul-to-soul experiences. The telephone, for middle-class American youth, has been part and parcel of their environment since birth, an assumed extension of their power to be personal and direct and immediate in relationships. Middle-aged parents find that their protests and their threats have little restraining effect upon a generation which has replaced the postage stamp with the "collect call." That generation's preference for the call thus may not be simply shiftlessness.

We understand the spoken word as more *personal* than other forms of communication and when we really wish "to reach" another person we employ it, but the concept "personal" needs some exploration. The scholars speak of the "interiorizing" power of the spoken word and that concept is central to our purpose, but it must be made clear that it is an interiorizing designed to open up and to reveal and to nurture health and wholeness, not one that is a centering into self. These dangers have been long spelled out by an intellectual culture framed by disciples of Kant and congenitally suspicious even of the word "subjective." We do not discount them. But see how limited and suffocating, if you will, is the power of the visual in contrast to sound.

The visual tends to exteriorize. It depersonalizes human relationships. For this reason kind and sensitive people do not stare at other persons. It reduces them to objects. Staring is rude. It can shatter insecure persons. The "staring" contest held in jest often has an unsettling effect. Indeed, it is ended by that person who gets most unsettled first. One or the other turns away in relief from that pressure.

The confrontation "eyeball to eyeball" does not suggest new depths of relationship or a suitable strategy for the little flock in the world or in its own councils, but rather, it proposes the use of personal power to contest and dismantle the personal. It was instinctive wisdom that, as children, we welcomed the sightless piano tuner who talked with us and we counted him our friend and ally. It was tragically otherwise with the deaf man who passed our sidewalk games morning and evening. We feared that silent figure, and his eye upon us backed us up away from him fearfully and quietly. If he became paranoid, it surely was in part his response to our fear.

So trust and its flowering in friendship is intimately related to communication and especially to the peculiar power which human speech possesses to search out and reveal the interior of life. But note the role of faith in all this even at the purely human level. Friendship flowers when we *believe* that what our friend chooses to tell us about himself, his life of feeling, value, aspiration—that is, his interior life—is true. There is no way for anyone to experience directly someone else's interiority. There is no way to make it visual, an outward phenomenon to be verified, something that is "literally" true, objectified in a way pleasing to the age of typography and visual analogy. Each one of us stands as a reigning sovereign over his own inner life. "Among men, who knows what a man is but the man's own spirit within him?" (I Corinthians 2:11).

We may elect in the freedom which marks our personhood, our likeness to God, to "open up" to someone else or to hide from someone else. The symbols we use of any sort, from raised eyebrow or autobiographical novel to the tenderest employment of human speech in the intimate whisper of love and loyalty may be used either way. That is, they may "reveal" the inner man or they may be a large and calculated deceit, employed to hide the inner man.

This is the point at which "faith" is demanded to nurture the relationship. The other human person in the human equation must decide which it is: revelation or concealment. Friendship is based upon the confidence that what our friend tells us about his interior is indeed true and honest insofar as he understands it. But there is no guarantee, no absolute proof. If there were, where would be the beauty in loyalty and the unfolding excitement in love's commitment? What another person tells us may be a great "put on" and, trusting him, we may be horribly mistaken and hurt. Nevertheless, trust that our friend *is* revealing his true self insofar as he is able and is not engaging in deliberate deceit is the one essential element in friendship. "Soul to soul, person to person. . . ." Father Ong phrases it clearly, "Personal relations demand interchange of personal interiors."

In this interchange the spoken word holds a primary place as a most precious and powerful agent. So the parent troubled by a letter from an absent child rejoices in the telephone. So lovers only write letters awaiting the day of personal reunion or to "convey word" they could not bear to say or hear face to face, so anxiety-ridden may be the self-revealing. Thus it is that a thoughtful person under ordinary circumstances would not dictate a letter of sympathy. The dictating, the secretary, the typewriter, each removes him further from the person he would reach personally, soul to soul. If he cannot go in person, a handwritten note, even when the handwriting makes it difficult to decipher the "literal" message, is more personal, that is, exposes more of the inner man, of love and caring. Your time, your energy, your body are more expended in the handwriting. It is nearer human speech, nearer the inner man or his essence. ". . . for the ear tests what is spoken as the palate savors food" (Job 34:3). "Soul to soul, person to person. . . ." That is all human enough. But what about the divine?

Spoken language is propelled by your own breath into another's ear and in thinking about it we begin to feel the perceptivity of a religious tradition which associates breath with spirit and spirit with the interiority of God. When we turn to that question we see the cruciality of human trust in that divine relation which flowers in religious faith.

If the interchange of personal interiors so indispensable to human personal relations rests upon trust and confidence, so also with the human-divine relationship. We no sooner finish Paul's incomparable ode on Christian love which is the thirteenth chapter of I Corinthians than we read from the same hand that "the Spirit explores everything," a truth put first, as we have, at the human level, asking, "Who knows what a man is but the man's own spirit within him?" Then Paul rushes on to say, "In the same way, only the spirit of God knows what God is," and to make the claim that "This is the Spirit we have received." Immediately the mystery and power and divine quality of human speech is noted as he concludes, "We *speak* these gifts of God in *words* found for us not in human wisdom but by the Spirit." Inspiration! "Inspirited," indeed! Interior to interior, person to person, and God to man and man to God. Adoration, thanksgiving, confession, instruction, and the whole orchestration of the church's life and the Christian's joy. Reality here, as in the interactionist model of social conscience, described by Robert Bellah, resides "not just in the object but in the subject and particularly in the relation between subject and object." And so, later on, Paul, protesting a too esoteric view of human speech, asks for that sort of language which "contains something by way of revelation, or enlightenment, or prophecy, or instruction" (I Corinthians 14).

So it is especially by human speech that person is revealed to person, interior to interior in rich exchange built on trust, but more, too! It is also the instrument of God's revelation. The Word made flesh suggests in part the actual "becoming" in which human speech participates.

This brings us directly to the *second aspect* of the nature of human speech which bears with particular relevance upon the life of feeling and faith. The first aspect we have been discussing describes the *interiorizing* power of the spoken word. We could summarize the second aspect which we now approach as the *creating* power of human speech. In effect we move along now to examine the claim that *human speech as the most immediate and lively form of language does not simply describe thoughts or events but participates in their creation.*

This second claim about the capacity of human speech to bring into existence what did not exist before leads us directly to a definition of the church which can be a guide for many a little flock in its search for new heart. However, we will not be ready for that definition if we do not first clarify where we stand on the age-old question.

When I was a child one of my brothers, ten years my senior and of a philosophical and reflective nature, would tease my mind with the question about the tree falling in the woods. "When a tree comes cracking down," he would ask, "and there is no one present with capacity to hear, is there any sound?" The common-sense answer was clear. Of course, the sound of the tree falling would be there even if there were no one present to hear it. That answer comes naturally to those deeply immersed in a visual manner of thinking about reality and truth. What is true and real is objective, "out there" somewhere independent of the viewer, existing apart from him and his viewing. However, that natural, common-sense "view" trembles when sound with its dynamic aliveness and transitory nature is questioned rather than sight. I have not found any philosopher or theologian who has dealt definitely with this favorite question and offered a clear-cut answer. So here I risk my own view that sound does not come into being apart from some instrument, mechanical or personal, with capacity to respond. This is equally true of human speech, except that the question is clouded by the fact that the speaker and the hearer can be the same person.

This ancient question about the tree in the woods is raised to emphasize that the word "speech" will be clearly inadequate all through this discussion if it suggests any lonely, isolated experience, the sort of "speech-making" where the response of the hearers is forgotten in the ego trip of the speaker and not recognized as an integral part of the whole experience. For our purposes we will think of human speech as the function of a larger community than "me, myself and I" and keep in mind the full range of human speaking and hearing, a magnificent, busy, two-way street. In describing these two characteristics of speech, its interiorizing power and its creating power, the interpersonal dimension is clearly an integral part.

Speech is a function of community, two persons or more. There is no interior revealed unless it is revealed to *someone* even as there is no sound without the human instrument to fill out the entire equation of stimulus and response. So the community of persons is creative of speech. *It is also created by speech.* The church is, indeed, a "Speech Event" dramatized by the story of Pentecost and recreated again and again when two or more persons gather with Christ in their hearts and Jesus on their lips. Remembering the power of human speech to search out and reveal the interior of life as well as its power to participate in the creation of thoughts and events, we are prepared to get a glimpse of what Ernst Fuchs means when he writes that "God's revelation consisted simply in God letting men state God's own problems in their language, in grace and judgment." [8]

So we are ready now to offer a working definition of the church and see its actuality in the local parish: "The church is a group of people engaged in all kinds of conversation about Jesus of Nazareth and about a host of related persons and events." That is the essence of Matthew

8. Ernest Fuchs, "The New Testament and the Hermeneutical Problem" in *New Frontiers in Theology, Volume II: The New Hermeneutic,* eds. Robinson and Cobb (New York: Harper and Row, 1964).

18:20: "For where two or three are gathered in my name there am I in the midst of them."

This definition deepens and its implications begin to unfold as we place upon it the tremendous weight of Christian witness and experience which claim that *only* as the two or three come together and engage in that conversation, that discourse about Jesus and the host of related persons and events, can Christ be known and identified. That unhiding, that revealing, that making of him present both for the nurture of the church and for his confrontation with the world is the measure and hallmark of his church wherever it appears, no matter how simple or elaborate, how justified or useless those extensions may be which persons build upon that human experience of Christian discourse.

To claim so much for such a modest community as the one we know as our local congregation or its primitive prototype moving along the road to Emmaus which, you will recall, was *"talking* together of all these things which had happened" (Luke 24:14, italics added) may appear presumptuous until we take a closer look at the nature of conversation, of human speech at work. Then we discover that the matter, the substance, the object that is over and beyond both parties to a conversation—which transcends them—is brought into their presence by their conversation about it. Conversation, like all forms of language, refers to something beyond it.

So this working definition of the church as "a community of Christian discourse" reflects the wisdom of scholars who remind us that we do not have thoughts somehow in the abstract and then call up human speech as we might summon a photographer to record what those thoughts are. Rather, human speech, like other forms of language, is an indispensable partner in the whole creative process. So in the broad life of the church, in its liturgy and in its mission, we experience the truth that "human speech as the most immediate and lively form of language does not simply describe thoughts or events but participates in their creation."

> For as the rain and the snow come down from heaven, and return not
> thither but water the earth, making it bring forth and sprout, giving
> seed to the sower and bread to the eater, so shall my word be that goes

forth from my mouth; it shall not return to me empty, but it shall accomplish that which I purpose, and prosper in the thing for which I sent it.

Isaiah 55:10–11

So it is that human speech with its dynamic temporality and instant claim does not simply point to divine reality or describe it, but it is in itself a creative power, or essential agency of such power.

Thus the critical change in contemporary thought from viewing truth as delivered in the past waiting to be uncovered to the understanding that truth is to be discovered lying not in the past but in the future. Here is the theological basis for the suggestion in an earlier chapter about the parish and its children. We recalled there Marshall McLuhan's criticism of education, which he says is programmed for instruction when it should be programmed for discovery. Could we enlarge that complaint now to apply to the whole of the little flock and suggest it should be programmed, as it is designed, for revelation. Thus it is that David James Randolph alerts us to the issue when he writes that Martin Heidegger "is convinced that a radical reinterpretation of language and being is absolutely necessary if we are to come to the truth. He has tugged at the slender roots of language, and the whole tree of theology shakes. The question may be put briefly. Does language 'point' or does it 'bring to expression'?"

That is a question of great academic interest, true. But it is also a matter of intense practical importance—central, crucial, unceasing—in every little flock of Christ, the contemporary, living manifestation of that oral institution, the church, now as always engaged in much speaking. How sobering is that theological tree-shaking when we consider the possibility of human speech as dynamic, creative power and when we hear the claim that "St. John was properly the first Christian theologian because he was overwhelmed by the spokenness of all meaningful happening." [9] Well, there is much "spokenness" in the church. It is an oral institution. That is its distinctive characteristic. But is there also much "meaningful happening"? That is the question.

---

9. Eugene Rosenstock-Huessy quoted in Harold Stahmer, *Speak That I May See Thee!* (New York: Macmillan, 1968), p. 1.

However, it must be remarked that the church as an oral institution or as a Speech Event or as a community of discourse does not turn away from the visual altogether. Quite to the contrary. Who can measure the value to faith of the visual symbols, the cross itself, or the colors of the church year or the written word in tract and Scripture? Nor does the church as Speech Event turn away from the other senses either. Who can measure the value to faith of the symbols of touch with its handshake of Christian affirmation or the Kiss of Peace, both of which rush in with the warm embrace of God's caring after words run out or stumble on our tongues? Who can measure the redeeming power in the bread broken and the cup poured out which convey that which is beyond any telling?

But all these nonspeech forms of language are refreshed and enlivened and filled with the *interiorizing* and *creative* power which speech possesses by the spoken word itself. Lest that assertion be discounted as religious rhetoric, it is instructive to note that in this new age of sound the written letter, the visual, is being used more and more simply to *confirm* a prior conversation or other personal encounter and to *retain its creative benefits* for those who participated in it and those who follow after them. Was it not so for the first disciples? "And he took bread, gave thanks, and broke it; and he gave it to them, *with the words:* 'This is my body' " (Luke 22:19, NEB; italics added). Was that not the experience of the truth to be extended into the centuries that the church is a community of Christian discourse, that where two or three are gathered *in his name,* Christ is there! O little flock, take heart!

·V·

Where There Is
a Steeple on the House

If the church is a community of Christian discourse with two or three gathered in Christ's name, then the little flock must *gather,* it must *meet* in order to be. It is damaging nonsense to propose such an omnipresent doctrine in Christ and such an abstract concept of his church that it all is seen in some vague way to splatter over the earth like a certain brand of paint.

In order for the church to exist, it must meet; in order for Christ to be present in that meeting, it must be "in his name." Until we are translated like Enoch, such a human endeavor will require a place and a time. Furthermore, that place and time will be special in the corporate life of faith. Speaking symbolically, there will be a steeple on the house where the church comes into being. (It could claim as its own the words of Robert Frost's poem: "A Steeple On The House.")

So then we make bold to assert that such a place and time is holy and sacred for Christians as other times and other places are not. There is an actual qualitative difference. Those who gather in his name furnish "the matrix," as Walter Ong phrases it, "the womb for his coming, as Mary's body once did. If the group calls and waits on him, he is there." [1]

This is not a conviction widely articulated among Protestants, if,

---

1. Walter J. Ong, *Presence of the Word* (New York: Simon & Schuster, 1970), p. 311.

indeed, it is held at all. We have been so distressed by the absurd idea that God is *only* in church or *only* in hushed conversations conducted in Gothic-shaped tones that we have affirmed he is everywhere. Of course he is! But our common-sense insistence that he is everywhere in general has suggested that he is, therefore, nowhere in particular! The truth is becoming clear that, if he is nowhere in particular, we are not apt to find him disclosed everywhere in general.

This secularization of the Almighty which arose as a corrective insistence that God is not the private property of religious persons and institutions was proposed as though it were a new and liberating idea, God of the Marketplace! But even King Solomon knew that. It was *when* Solomon was standing in front of the altar with his hands spread out toward heaven, it was *when* he was in a most holy place and in a most holy posture, that he prayed: "Heaven itself, the highest heaven cannot contain thee; how much less this house that I have built."

But an age of modern Christian secularity, morally eager to make all common things holy, has inadvertently tended to make all holy things common. Such an age must hear more of Solomon's prayer:

> Yet attend to the prayer of supplication of thy servant, O Lord my God; listen to the cry and prayer which thy servant utters before thee, that thy eyes may ever be upon this house day and night, this place of which thou didst say, "It shall receive my name"; . . .
>
> II Chronicles 6

So the Almighty and Holy God, whom the highest heaven cannot contain, much less the churches which we build for worship and the times we set apart for the conversation of holiness, does particularly and uniquely enter those times and spaces. "For where two or three have met together in my name, I am there among them" (Matthew 18:20, NEB).

The creative power of human speech is thus splendidly employed by the Eternal God. He will not abridge our freedom but when we talk together about him and his wonderful Event, he enters our experience by the grace of the instruments which he has given us. What a transforming sense of awe would fill our time and place of worship if we held a lively faith in his particular Presence there, if we truly believed that his eye was upon "this house day and night, this place of which thou didst say, 'It shall receive my name.' "

So consider this urgent conviction: the special time and place are sacred where we meet for conversation about Jesus and that host of related persons and events. They possess the particularity of holiness because Christ is there in a special way.

Not all life and all experience are equally sacred. To secularize special places even with the good intent of a democratic leveling of the sacred and the secular is a killing blight on human unfolding in our time. It is a myth slavishly followed by all too much of mainline Protestantism in America. It hides rather than exalts the single unique function of the church, public worship.

Again a fresh look at the singular power of human speech may help us work through this spiritual stalemate which has tarred our places and times of worship with the commonplace. When that is done, when the church in effect repudiates the steeple on its house, its capacity is diminished to be an instrument of change both personal and public, to be an instrument whereby God alters human awareness.

We have drawn out two lines of thought about human speech, its interiorizing power and its creative power. The first of these with some of its almost endless and fruitful ramifications and uses is well acknowledged and experienced in our culture. The exploration and use of its power in discussion groups, in psychotherapy, both group and individual, in conferences, aided and abetted by the instruments of an electronic age is a first giant step out of the limitations imposed by a visual culture into one with expanding appreciation for the larger world of sound. These employments are widely used in the church and have helped there, as elsewhere, in building up and deepening human relationships. Every local congregation, for example, needs committee chairpersons who develop specific practical skills of group interaction. All that illustrates the interiorizing power of human speech.

However, I believe much of the contemporary church is stuck there, spinning its wheels in an endless exploration of human interiority, of affirming and building up community in general and specializing in encounter, person to person. So the parish newspaper of a New England church carried a very strongly phrased article by a young woman

member of the congregation seriously proposing that public worship as
such be abandoned altogether because it was evident that the helpful
part of the Sunday morning experience was the Coffee Hour. She is not
alone in this feeling. The Coffee Hour experience, the friendly employment of the interiorizing power of speech, how beautiful it is and
how refreshing and helpful it often can be. But alas, I have had much
of the best of that "Coffee Hour experience" in a laundromat, sharing
privileged conversation with a stranger under the freeing and protective covering of anonymity while we watched the machines spin and
shared the pleasure of the fresh wash.

The church Coffee Hour experience will run out into the laundromat experience if the "interiorizing" of speech is limited to the
avowedly human exchange, good as that may be. The church has
resources beyond that; it has purpose in "meeting" over and above
chatting pleasantly or talking most earnestly or, as they say, "handling
conflict," about everything under the sun. It is concerned, one might
counter, not with everything under the sun but with everything *over*
the sun and all creation, with the source and end of being. The steeple
on the house is symbolic of this transcendental concern. Openness to
one another can end in an exchange of emptiness if its purpose is not
to participate, as human speech may be used to help us to do, in
calling into our midst Him whose glory the sun itself does declare.

That experience may well come about in a laundromat but, if it
does, then that becomes a sacred place. But that experience will remain spasmodic and embryonic and undernourished without the declaration of its nature by the identified community of faith and apart
from the discipline and sustenance offered by that community. "What
therefore you worship as unknown, this I proclaim to you" (Acts
17:23, RSV). This was Paul's opportunity at Athens, and, as we shall
contend in the final chapter, this is the contemporary church's missionary opportunity. For there are many such laundromats and many
such conversations all around the world where the implicit Christ
remains hidden until he is declared, that is, until the *creating* power of
human speech, as well as its interiorizing power, is engaged.

The church Coffee Hour, standing alone with the doors to the sanctuary locked and the worshiping congregation limited to the Fellow-

ship Hall encounter, would soon suffer the same impoverishment as that of the men of Athens and the visitors to the laundromat. It is an undernourishment not to be ended by good intentions and loving concern at the human level; far too deep is man's contradictory nature and too narrow is his natural interest. Such is the poverty of many an American congregation fluent in Coffee Hour and committee but frozen in proclamation and prayer, excelling in management by objective but ignorant of Scripture and floundering in the liturgy.

The interiorizing power of speech alone is not enough. The church as an effective oral institution must couple that power to the creating power of speech. The special discourse which makes the church the church, discourse about the historical Jesus and all that associated and glorious company of persons and events, is an instance of the creating power of human speech linked dynamically to its interiorizing power.

That is precisely the nature of public worship. It is interior to interior because it is creative of the divine Presence. The liturgy is the instrument of that creating, the liturgy which Franz Rosenzweig [2] described so gracefully howbeit with a metaphor of sight rather than sound, as "the reflector which focuses the sunbeams of eternity in the small circle of the year." That focusing is achieved with the miracle of human speech, a kind of human-divine conversation we call worship. The hymns, the Scripture, the responses, the preaching and the praying—here are people formally engaged in that discourse which promises Christ's coming. That is why the time and space set aside for Christian discourse are sacred and special. But, if they are not reserved with the *expectation* of his Coming, the hindrance to the miracle of his Presence is very large. If the building is regarded as any other public auditorium and if the assembling is for just another lecture or concert and if the time is resented or resisted—what then! Hence the arrogant or hapless futility of good intention in much so-called innovative worship, developed in response to an awareness of emptiness in public worship but in ignorance of the fact that the absence was Christ himself. All is further compounded by the intellectual and emotional sterility which ensues whenever the Word in Scripture or song or sermon

2. Nahum Glatzer and Franz Rosenzweig in Harold Stahmer, *Speak That I May See Thee* (New York: Macmillan, 1968), p. 253.

is emasculated by the presuppositions of a visual culture and its
curiously *literate* ignorance.

Reestablishing the support and encouragement which a special
place, a House with a Steeple, provides may be the genius and contribution of the Age of Sound to the fulfillment of the Great Commission. Indeed, it is time to note the inadequacy of the title of this
chapter to suggest its theme. The church needs not only a house—and
one with a steeple—but it needs a bell in the steeple. The reality
symbolized by the steeple is energized by sound. The local church
finds its true Heart as it participates in the creative power of sound, of
human speech, in being essentially an oral institution.

For "Sound of itself generates a sense of mystery," writes Father
Ong:

> Unlike time and space, which may or may not suggest activity, sound of
> itself, as an ongoing phenomenon, registers the actual use of power.
> Moreover, sound . . . is a manifestation of an interior. Voice, for man
> the paradigm of all sound, manifests the actual use of power by the most
> interior of interiors, a person. . . . This fact is critical in the Hebraic-
> Christian tradition, where God himself is personal. . . . It is impossible
> to be reverent to a thing simply as a thing.[3]

So the excitement for the future of faith is immediately at hand, it
is as close as a generation reared on the telephone and pleased with a
new tape-recorder. It is linked with technological advance, for who
can guess the inventive possibilities for the unfolding of a new age of
faith in a renewed age of sound as generations rise up to follow our
own who are not trussed in the binding of the typed page and its ex-
teriorizing of experience and who have accepted the mystery and miracle of modern communication media as natural extension of person.
Herein lies the basis for new optimism about the awakening of faith
which rests at the tip of our tongues. "For the faith that leads to righteousness is in the heart, and the confession that leads to salvation is
upon the lips" (Romans 10:10).

John Macquarrie, reviewing Heidegger's thought, writes: "Man
remains unique as the existent, the place of openness among all the be-

3. Walter J. Ong, *Presence of the Word* (New York: Simon & Schuster, 1970), p. 163.

ings." And elsewhere Heidegger makes clear his conviction that only language affords the possibility of standing in that opening.[4] That is a theological conviction complementary to the view of such a different sort of Christian scholar as Kenneth Scott Latourette who, in reviewing Christian history, believed the evidence that newness in Christianity does not come from intelligence and logic-proof arguments but from "souls who have opened themselves to Him and been made great by the touch of his Spirit."[5]

The resistance of modern man to that touch and to that conversation through which it may come is very great. The refusal of many Christian persons to entertain for even a moment the idea that the time and place reserved for worship are qualitatively different, special, sacred, is symptomatic of the exceedingly deep and hidden resistance to the divine touch. Places of worship are leveled or neglected in the name of great humanitarian causes, and times of worship are made casual and common under the guise of attacking other people's hypocrisy. Those who scorn the places and secularize the time often do so in some righteous press for the relevancy of faith.

How much that is deeper and more profoundly crucial for love, justice, and peace may be lost in the process. Robert Bellah, no campmeeting evangelist but professor of sociology first at Harvard and now at the University of California, writes that "The experience of worship should produce an influx of life and power, a feeling of wholeness, of the grace of God, of being at the still center of the turning wheel. . . ." He goes on to suggest that, if worship doesn't "work," it may not be because it is "irrelevant" but because "a modern straight type is apt to be in the grip of powerful unconscious fantasies that repeat themselves endlessly but get nowhere. . . . It is just because he is on such a bad trip, not because he is so 'mature' that he cannot let down his defenses enough to participate meaningfully in an act of worship."[6]

4. Gerhard Ebeling, *On Prayer,* tr. by James W. Leitch (Philadelphia: Fortress, 1966), p. 19.
5. Kenneth Scott Latourette, "Missions Tomorrow" in *South East Asia Journal of Theology,* p. 114.
6. Robert N. Bellah, *Beyond Belief* (New York: Harper & Row, 1970), p. 211.

It takes a great deal of courage to let those defenses down and to risk being open to another person. When one's self-assurance is more a matter of astute outward management than inward reality, the resistance to searching human conversation is often very strong. If we are frightened into self-justification by the risk of invitation to free and open *human* conversation, how futile is the hope that we will participate easily in divine conversation. We need tremendous support and encouragement—the sort offered by that special house marked by a steeple and set aside and reserved for that demanding encounter. It is not surprising to discover the close association in New Testament Greek of the terms for intercession and prayer with those for meeting and ordinary discourse. Harold Stahmer tells us that "Plato once used the same term to describe the boldness with which pirates board a ship . . . elements of encounter, address, engagement, struggle are equally present." [7]

The so-called "straight types" have no corner on the fears which keep us from that engagement and struggle. All persons need all the support they can find to venture in that experience. Such is the service of a special place, a sacred place. A friend recently reported taking her husband and children to visit the church of her childhood. They did not ride a cloud to some airily invisible or generalized place. They drove an automobile on hard-surfaced roads to an existing city where people live and work and hunted up a particular building which the children recognized from afar as a church. There was, perhaps, a steeple. And they opened "the door and found the people," even on a Tuesday afternoon, for it was filled, she said, with all the church ghosts of her childhood memory and there lovingly she introduced them to her children—the oral tradition encouraged and revived by the gracious help of a special place to visit. The community of faith, already meagerly experienced by those children, was thus enlarged and reinforced.

So there are two corollary truths about that house with a steeple on it which many a parish church sustains at no little sacrifice. *The first concerns its importance to the parish itself.* It is true that many church

7. Harold Stahmer, *Speak That I May See Thee!* (New York: Macmillan, 1968), p. 31.

buildings have become occasions for sin. Whenever they become "ends" in themselves they are corrupted. In appropriate revolt against that distortion of a special place, many of us have never understood their importance as means of support and identity for communities of faith. The community does not exist in the abstract. It becomes "embodied" in place and time when it meets. The nature of that embodiment, tent or cathedral, corner of a warehouse or a rural building in carpenter gothic, is important. It has effect upon those who call it their church.

Philip Slater's claim, presented in the first few pages of this book, about the desire for community frustrated by American culture, is for a community which is a "total and visible entity." [8] The local church *can* be that kind of community. The building where it meets is part of its visibility. Its values are reflected in that building. Many American churches are hardly distinguishable from the suburban high school, and others reflect the neglect suffered at the hands of a generation whose suspicions of "American materialism" have given idealistic rationalizations for not sweeping the walk or painting the front door.

That house with a steeple will be felt by the people to be very special. It will be filled with such signs as to provoke a sacred memory and call into being a sacred hope. It should be beautiful in some true sense, not only with beauty as an aesthetic category but as a moral category, not only the beauty of traditional symbol and sound, but the *beauty of hard use to serve the secular community in which it is placed*. It will possess that rare beauty of a threshold made smooth by many feet and kept shining by much scrubbing and loving care.

This house will be "special" with many signs "that a soul is coming in the flesh." It will assist in provoking the sense of awe which opens being to Being if it is especially reserved in some part to be the scene of life's most profound and searching moments. It is in that house with a steeple that the little flock will gather for the baptism of infants with the entire congregation speaking of their willingness and intent to surround that child with love's own nurturing. There will lovers come to declare publicly their commitment. There the little flock will

8. Philip E. Slater, *The Pursuit of Loneliness: American Culture at the Breaking Point* (Boston: Beacon Press, 1971), p. 5.

bring their dead for a glorious Te Deum and a final Benediction. However, the sacredness of the special time and place for meeting has been eroded by those who do not believe much in "meeting" and who regard their religion as a highly personal affair. So the Bible is read silently and privately and thus never fully heard because it is an instrument for oral use by a community; so prayer is limited to its silent and personal dimension and its explosion in the Great Amen of the whole congregation is never set loose; so infant baptism is seen as magic or personal dedication of parents suitable for a private garden and missed as the praise of the whole church in all times and places for that divine love which precedes our lovableness and is not a response to our obedience; and so the undertaker's parlor becomes a place of convenience for the private pain of separation and the bereft enter into commercial contract with those who obscure death and miss that great company who assemble to affirm the Resurrection. So profound has been our dismantling of the steeple in our culture and the parishes nurtured beneath them that Forest Lawn Cemetery, with chapels for weddings as well as euphemized funerals, has become a sort of national cathedral of the emerging national religion.

Of course, one of the great obstacles to community is the mobile nature of American culture. Middle-class families scarcely stay long enough in one place to have two children baptized in the same congregation, let alone be buried in the graveyard of the church where they were nurtured in the faith as a child. But here again the new age of sound may lift us out of this distressing sense of discontinuity and ease our reluctance to put roots down in one community of faith knowing that we will only have to rip them out with the next managerial shift.

Persons in Western culture are so mobile that we have assumed community cannot last long even for those who find it in the local church. However, it would not take much to identify and make specific member congregations of a network of churches which share similar styles of parish life and expression. In many cases there is greater affinity between congregations across denominational lines than between those with denominational ties. Modern communication media, used to bind motels of similar quality across the nation, could be used to bind similar congregations together and serve the needs of its mobile members. Advance notice of the stranger's arrival assists both motel and customer. Similar notice could serve both established congregation and transient visitors and newcomers, hastening the welcome and easing the strangeness which often hinders full participation. Many a traveling housewife has felt frustrated and lonely when she has entered a strange supermarket and has had to spend a half hour finding a quart of milk. How delighted she is when she discovers the branch of a familiar chain—especially if she or her family is hungry. She feels right at home. Here uniformity is not constricting but liberating. She is freed to shop rather than to hunt.

Early one drizzly darkling winter Sunday morning my wife and I entered a Jewish synagogue in downtown Birmingham, Alabama, in our search for the Baptist Church of the Covenant which was reputed to be worshiping there. We were strangers in a strange land. Neither the building nor the hour offered the comfort of familiarity. But immediately upon entering an older man who looked like any half dozen wonderful church-type saints we have known from coast to coast greeted us and handed us a hymnal. It was the familiar red-bound *Pilgrim Hymnal* used by our own congregation more than two thousand miles away. Familiarity eased our timidity and within moments we were deeply engaged in that service, in that particular instance of Christian discourse. But how much we all need help over the initial resistance and inertia, the much prayed-about "wanderings of mind"!

A Special Place in Time and Space and Sound offers support and encouragement to the community of faith itself, at home and abroad, which often meets only to find itself tongue-tied or trivial. How often we display that perverse skill Hawthorne phrased so well in *The Scarlet Letter:* "It is singular how long a time often passes before words embody things; and with what security two persons, who choose to avoid a certain subject, may approach its very verge, and retire without disturbing it." [9] We need help. If I were a Roman Catholic, I would wonder if the help offered is sometimes really helpful. I would wonder if more had been lost than gained in shifting the language of the Mass

9. Nathaniel Hawthorne, *The Scarlet Letter* (New York: Washington Square Press, 1970), p. 235.

to the vernacular. I am sure I would wonder about that loss if I were an English-speaking American attending Mass in Tokyo or Istanbul! However, world travelers have warned me that such an observation is much too simplistic because there is as much difference, they say, between Chinese Latin and German Latin as there is between Chinese and German!

"A spire and belfry coming on the roof" are significant not only for the congregation which gathers beneath that roof but also for the secular city which benefits by a special place and time set aside by the community of faith. The steeple stretching upward is a most urgent symbol and witness to rise up in the midst of the whole community of mankind. The moral indignation expressed about expenditure of money for a church building should be balanced by intense concern about a community which has no one expressing anything loftier than its own commonality. There is much scandal in church buildings, unused buildings, ugly buildings, buildings which do not proclaim anything of Christ and his Spirit! But, alas, there is no poverty in the secular city more to be feared than the poverty which will ensue when there is no sacred place and time in the midst of it and no soaring spire to contradict and challenge its human assumptions.

"Until the Gothic style," Kenneth Clark tells us, "men had thought of buildings as weight upon the ground. . . . Now by the devices of the Gothic style—the shaft with its cluster of columns, passing without interruption into the vault and the pointed arch—he could make stone seem weightless; the weightless expression of his spirit." [10] There has been much humanitarian concern and not a little of human nonsense about the scandal of European villages—or even Canadian—enduring in apparent poverty with great cathedrals rising out of their slums. But can any village which elects to build a great cathedral to express its love for God be considered "poor"? Is it "poorer" than a wealthy manicured suburb whose cathedral is a school and whose corridor for prayer is a freeway slashing through unseen slums and washing away acres of rich topsoil? And where does concern for the "poor" arise if it does not come from the presence of that Spirit

10. Kenneth Clark, *Civilisation* (New York: Harper & Row, 1970), p. 59.

which the great cathedral has continued through the ages? There have been and there remain grave abuses and perversions to be lamented and corrected in the imbalance between buildings and souls, between art and soup, between hardware and persons. But there is today the need for what a house with a steeple on it and a bell in the steeple may provide.

Consider the situation in the city where I live, as described by a newspaper journalist. After picturing "some nice little vegetable gardens" which are flourishing in the regained People's Park, the journalist continues.

> But half way across the park is a rough excavation four or five feet deep and about 20 feet across.
> A fire burns in one corner. A filthy mattress lies uncovered on the dirt; the place is strewn with trash and old dirty clothes.
> Several youths and girls cluster about the fire drinking wine. One young man goes into a nearby portable toilet. Chunks of broken concrete are thrown against it from the pit—the occupant shouts in anger.[11]

Shall the nearby church sell out? Convert its building to other uses or tear it down? Shall the members join the evacuation parade led by former members who have fled to higher and more distant ground? Or, is there an important witness to a persistently well-groomed building, wide open doors for Bach concerts on a baroque organ which fill the church with an odd assortment of street people and an occasional whiff of marijuana? Amid the scores of mimeographed propaganda sheets and posted notices, obscene and otherwise, there floats every summer on nearby Telegraph Avenue a colorful sheet with a message in large bright letters: FOLLOW A RED BALLOON and an announcement about a "program of exploration and discovery" for any child. It is believed that any grubby, little, undernourished child of the children of the streets who follows that red balloon into that special house with the steeple and is welcomed by a people made beautiful by their experience there will discover unknown options quite beyond a dreary dragging of the days from one protest to the next.

A special place in time and space is a witness; and the worship of

11. *Oakland Tribune*, June 27, 1972.

the community of faith is always *public* worship. And it is not true that "they pray best together who first pray alone," but quite the reverse. The church, an oral institution, a Speech Event, cannot read the Bible silently or engage in personal prayers and really read the Bible or truly pray, for both are only half done unless it is a community affair, interior to interior, and human speech is engaged in the doing. That takes a special place in time and space . . . but it always takes "special sound"—a voice speaking and an ear hearing—toward the unfolding of that truth. The electronic age is especially designed by Him who is resolved that his Word shall not return to Him void.

·VI·

Where the Doors
Open Outward

There is the suspicion lurking in my heart that if we were to submit the foregoing pages of this book to the scrutiny of our Lord, he might quote his own sermon to us and ask, as in Matthew 5:47: ". . . if you salute only your brethren, what more are you doing than others?" That question presses as an even more penetrating critique when phrased by J. B. Phillips: ". . . if you exchange greetings only with your own circle, are you doing anything exceptional? Even the pagans do as much."

A few years ago when our church budget needed trimming, our congregation decided to cut down on advertising. That was a mistake. The motivation was honorable. Advertising felt like boasting if it were designed for those outside the church to read. If it were for our own people, it was a luxury. It was "exchanging greetings only with your own circle." So we cut way back on advertising and never a cent from missions. Or so we thought! But we actually cut back on missions in cutting back on advertising.

Recently two lay persons, one an artist and one an advertising executive, worked up some new paid advertising for our parish in addition to utilizing the many opportunities for free publicity in the various media. We wanted one to express our desire to exchange greetings outside our own circle. It looked like this:

WE'RE PERFECTLY WILLING NOT TO NOTICE YOU

If you want to visit our church and sit alone, **welcome**. If you want to say nothing, **welcome**. But if you don't want to sit alone, and if you don't want to say nothing, **welcome**. We'll sit with you. We'll listen to you.

WELCOME... on any terms you want.

First Congregational Church (UCC), Berkeley
Dana & Channing Way   Call 848-3696 day or night
Public Worship 10 a.m. Sundays—Tune KRE (1400AM)

We wanted one which would be honest about our view of the Bible. It looked like this:

28 REASONS you might like us (and one reason you might not)

We have something for all — exceptional preaching • 10 a.m Sunday worship • crib care • weekday study groups • adult choir • high school center • weekly communion service • Boy Scout troop • active couples' clubs • boys' choir • sr. citizens' group • monthly pastoral ministry • lecture series • toddlers' class • choir • women's concerts • pre-school class • girls' choir • weekly prayer ser- groups • instrumental ensemble • library • grade vice • social concerns seminar • seminars • chil- school classes • sermon group • bell dren's choir • poetry service on choir • Sunday KRE-1400 AM at 10 a.m. • But — we don't take the Bible literally, just seriously. Can you live with that?

First Congregational Church (UCC), Berkeley
Dana & Channing Way   Call 848-3696 day or night

He designed Another to suggest our experimental ecumenicity at the local level. It looked like this:

One about Christian education brought back some of our own families who had strayed after the summer holiday. It also helped some children bring their parents. It looked like this:

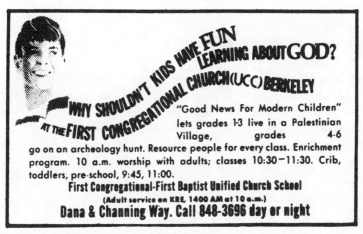

Practical American-style advertising is one way the little flock can break out of its own circle. It is the mildest sort of beginning but it can lead to all kinds of creative involvements with the world. It would take another occasion to relate some individual and corporate methods appropriate for those who rightly seek to break out of parish and ecclesiastical circles and be obedient to Christ as participants in society. But it is of interest that the words in Ephesians about breaking out of your own little circle and venturing to encounter people who are outside the family, beyond the parish boundaries, is immediately followed with the injunction, "you are to be perfect, like your heavenly Father." Can it be that this is the secret of God the Father, the divine Creator, and to be like him is to participate in his endless creativity? Is this the purpose of that freedom which marks our own being as in God's image? And is that being fulfilled when we break out of the familiar circle, responding to some mighty spiritual instinct like a youth drawn from the family circle to embrace a new love?

So every local church stands in mortal peril when it mistakenly views its own life as an end in itself. Don Benedict, speaking some years ago at the annual meeting of the Metropolitan Missionary Society of Los Angeles, phrased this widely acknowledged truth more pungently: "When you see church after church closed in the inner city, God is saying to that church you were not the church anyway. You were a club. You really wouldn't let anyone in the door. You guys had a neat club, and a neat little racket but you wouldn't open the door." So the dangers of parish navel-gazing are well noted. But that is nothing new. We have been hearing about this danger for two decades and have responded with the "relevancy game" where the central refrain has been, "See, Christian friends, far and wide, my parish, my church, my witness is more relevant than yours!"

Now that our young people are getting caught up in Zen Buddhism and Yoga and other spiritual religions and meditation cults, the "relevancy" wing of the church is running scared. The alarm was sounded by an exceptionally keen and courageous leader of my own very "relevant" denomination to a meeting of our churches when he described part of the faith crisis as a turning of the faith inward. "All across our land," he said, "people are turning their faith inward. But this privatization of faith has its dangers, the most serious being that the faith will be taken over by the culture in which we live." [1]

It is well to mark those dangers but they depend upon what one means by inwardness and from what one is turning. It is a warning to be heeded, but thoughtfully. It is my conviction, which I believe Katagiri also shares, that in the liberal churches which have long been resolved and committed to show forth a "relevant" faith, some inwardness has been long overdue in order to discover adequate resources for faith's outwardness. But, alas, those resources are not to be discovered by careless ignorance of two thousand years of Christian history and of the other Egypts and Israels in and out of which we have wandered or been thrust.

Recently at two different but largely attended conferences of a mainline Protestant denomination, the sacrament of the Lord's Supper has been "used" to illustrate the world's hunger and in one instance was framed about with the reading of an American Indian folk tale. How shall our eyes be opened in the breaking of the bread if it be separated from that Scripture which is its wheat and its yeast? The world's hunger is a noteworthy, comprehensive, outward-reaching concern of the church and of all humane persons and it is to be hoped and believed that those who have been fed at the Lord's table will be more sensitive than ever to that moral and painful injustice. But to turn Holy Communion into an allegory and the Lord's table into an illustration of scarcity is to see the faith taken over by the culture indeed! But it is taken over through an effort at "relevancy" rather than as a consequence of inwardness!

Nonetheless it may be argued that we have spent too much time in these chapters on the refurbishing of the local church and that long ago we should have turned to the relationship of that community of faith to the world around it and beyond it. This emphasis has been a matter of deliberate design. It seeks in part to heed the warning and

---

1. Mineo Katagiri, assistant to the president, United Church of Christ, Ailomar, May 18, 1972.

profit by the experience of the early church. W. D. Davies, in his excellent and useful book *Invitation to the New Testament,*[2] reminds us that, "As the church spread further and further into the Graeco-Roman world, it became more and more necessary for it to secure its base, as it were. Just as an army can go too far away from its base, so as to jeopardize its reinforcements, so the primitive church could have jeopardized its very existence by removing itself too far from that event which was its foundation." The energetic center of that event, of course, was "the Word made flesh, that is, in the historically real Jesus." The church, not as theological abstraction or political block, but as specific community, submitting to the discipline of Scripture and the grace of the sacraments, is the base from which we dare not be severed. The church must understand and feel what it may be like to be Christ's flock. But that flock is not an end in itself; it is a nurturing center for that community of Christians which only lives as it also moves out of its own circle to salute strangers everywhere, demonstrating again the kinship of fire and church, for as one lives by burning, the other lives by mission. Indeed, the words of Jesus, "Fear not, little flock," [3] appear in the context of the church's conviction that it was the nucleus of a coming new order of righteousness.

Virginia Satir claims that she and her colleagues uniformly discovered that families which were truly vital and nurturing to their members were invariably *"linked to society in an open and hopeful way."* That truth is of considerable interest to the little flock which may so seek new heart *within* its own life that it never finds it. The energy for new heart may lie in large measure quite beyond its own boundaries.

Repeatedly in these chapters we have found encouragement and incredible enlargement from the letter to the Ephesians with its warm pastoral admonition about anger and forgiveness and loving one another in the community of faith as Christ has loved us. But Ephesians

2. W. D. Davies, *Invitation to the New Testament* (New York: Doubleday, 1969), pp. 82–83.
3. "Have no fear, little flock; for your Father has chosen to give you the Kingdom. Sell your possessions and give in charity. Provide for yourselves purses that do not wear out, and neverfailing treasure in heaven, where no thief can get near it, no moth destroy it. For where your treasure is, there will your heart be also. Be ready for action, with belts fastened and lamps alight" (Luke 12:32–35, NEB).

is no handbook on how to get along in the parish! It boldly declares God's purpose "to unite all things in heaven and earth" and announces that once and for all and forever the dividing wall of enmity between Gentile and Jew was laid low by Christ. So this great epistle serves us well in underscoring this quality which must be central to the little flock, for if it is Christ's flock, it must be *linked to society in an open and hopeful way.*

That society is composed of many cities, both holy and secular, and many cultures both urban and rural, old and new, East and West, and it has been and continues to be fed by many truly inspired philosophers and teachers who do not bear the imprimatur of Rome, much less of 475 Riverside Drive, New York City! If the little flock is going to be linked to that society in an open and hopeful way, it must discover a fresh humility sustained by deeply renewed certainties.

From the particular point of view of a parish minister who constantly deals with the hope of ordinary people for a new and better society both at home and abroad, and who also constantly encounters the resistance of many such persons to the missionary motif of Christianity, it appears that, if the local church is to be linked to society in an open and hopeful way, it needs to incorporate into its being the most profound dimensions of the overarching theme of the epistle to the Ephesians, which is *unity.*

The fullness toward which the *whole creation* moves is unity in Christ. As the little flock seeks to link itself to the whole world in an open and hopeful way, this epistle urges the implications of unity, first *theologically,* and second *practically.* We will follow that lead in this chapter and consider first the theological implications of "unity in Christ" which leads us immediately to Christology, reflection on the nature of Christ. Then we will move on to the practical implications of "unity in Christ" for the life of the church in and for the whole world.

First, then, Christology: Who is this Christ to whom we are commissioned to make all nations disciples? Many open-minded and broadly educated persons in our congregations find it difficult to relate themselves in any religiously missionary fashion to people outside the parish, whether they be next door or across the seas, not because they have such a broad view of Christ, as is often supposed, but quite to the contrary it seems to me, because they have such a narrow and limited view.

If we believe that Christ is encountered and known *only* in Jesus, the teacher of Galilee, then it does sound like ingratiating exclusiveness and is a dogma which makes everyone but Christians "not OK." But here again the writer of the letter to the Ephesians is addressing us, for he refuses to get bogged down in any such religious provincialism as that. Like Jeremiah arguing with the false prophets, he is saying, "God is greater than you think." To him Christ is not limited to Palestine and His work is not restricted to ending the ancient animosity between Jew and Gentile. Christ is not even limited to the Galilean teacher, the Jesus of history. To be sure, Christ was made evident for the writer of this epistle *in* Palestine and *through* the person of Jesus of Nazareth and his power was effective in removing the barrier between Jew and Gentile; the eternal Christ was there *experienced* but not there *confined!*

In this gracious epistle, as in St. John's Gospel, Christ is understood as being identical with the integrating power of the universe. That power is greater than you think. It is love!—personalized, intense, present, experienced in Jesus to be sure, but also and as well this Christ was from before the worlds were framed: "He was in the beginning with God . . . in Him was life and the life was the light of men."

Many a local church might be set free to engage with incredibly multiplied energy in its missionary task if it would seriously encounter this early Christian whose views break forth from the pages of Ephesians and who refused to settle for any narrow or sectarian view of Christ. The Christ to whom he would bring the nations—or at least to whom he would bring this one gathering in Ephesus—is clothed in garments far more universal in style and far more adjustable to distant climes and strange customs than any designed solely for the streets of Jerusalem or found under the stars of Bethlehem.

If we are to relate to all of society *everywhere* in "an open and hopeful way" and, as modern persons, declare wholeheartedly the exclusive claims of Christ to the world of Islam or to the followers of Buddha or to the disciples of Marx, we must move not with a provincial Jesus but with the universal Christ there incarnate! That Christ has no parley with time and is not hindered by place. He is one whose life and death and resurrection address the universal situation of all mankind, struggling against the destructive power of self-interest, and pressing, as though possessed by a hidden love, toward that Kingdom where the loveliest intimations of what life might be are fulfilled.

That cosmic Christ may well be no stranger to those who have heard love's song beside other seas than Galilee and beheld its sacrifice on other hills than Calvary. That Christ is no stranger to other metaphors and idioms, and stands, for example, at the doorway of the Castle from predynastic Egypt to Kafka as well as at the entrance gate of the biblical Kingdom. That Castle, found in many centuries and religions, has symbolized for others the ideal human existence marked by "freedom and beauty, by light and love." [4] The rooms of that Castle when opened up by Christ are radiant with every color of the rainbow and there are strong and lovely songs in every language, as at Pentecost, streaming from its parapets.

However, as this cosmic view of Christ dawns on the modern little flock which has been prepared for it better than any previous generation through widespread secular education and by the tragic absurdities of our wars and the shrinking of the globe and the ensuing experience with and respect for other persons and cultures and religions, we are tempted to devise a human response by selecting the best elements from many faiths and creating a synthetic religion, a sort of spiritual Esperanto. This approach fails truly to recognize that to acknowledge the *universality* of Christ is not to alter the *singularity* of Christ. Christ is the eternal principle, the Word, the Logos, the character and being and energy and expression of God himself. There are not many partial Christs to be gathered together and synthesized, but one Christ to be discovered through the many partial instruments of revelation in many times and places.

Therefore, the resource needed for Christian mission is not propaganda but excitement about *our* experience of Christ in *our encounter with Jesus* coupled with an incredible and beautiful openness to hear how others have met him.

4. Malachi Martin, *New Castle* (New York: E. P. Dutton, 1974).

Christian mission in a world grown small and volatile desperately calls for churches which are linked to society in "an open and hopeful way," because the crucial instrument of mission in such a world is discourse and dialogue, not propaganda and persuasion. Christian mission in our age as in every other age is participation in that mutual unhiding which must mark communication in the parish church and which is the secret tool and essence of biblical revelation.

In a world of discovery and surprise and growth, in a creation of infinite possibilities, shall religion be frozen in some one place and culture for all time and eternity? "In Christ," this epistle declares, "the whole building is bonded together and *grows* into a holy temple in the Lord" (italics added). The word is not synthesis but mutation, growing and changing—glory into glory.

Malachi Martin, to whom we owe the Castle image, believes there was a moment of such spiritual sharing and trust in religious history about 1000 A.D. There was then in Spain and southern France "a commingling of knowledge in the spirit. . . . It was Islam's finest hour," he writes. "And Christians, Jews and Muslims learned briefly how to walk in their universe as if beside a see-through lattice giving onto divinity, present, ever-loving, making all things worthwhile."

Perhaps the Almighty has called religiously tolerant Christians of our time, who pride themselves on their openness but who everywhere seem to have lost a sense of mission about the faith itself and who have increasingly regarded missionary evangelism as an effrontery to other cultures—perhaps he has prepared such a religious community for the high task of restoring that "commingling of knowledge in the spirit." Perhaps such a community is called to take the initiative, employing world dialogue and international discourse to dig beneath the liberal Christian's commitment to world peace, for example. There it may discover that universal Christ who is the fountainhead of all peace. Perhaps, as at least one historian of religion believes, the next radical mutation in theology will emerge from such an encounter of the West with Asia symbolized by the Buddha. Indeed, perhaps God's judgment and hence his prompting is already falling around many middle-class Protestant parishes in the fragmenting spiritual struggle of their youth who finally had to turn to the East for instruction in prayer, unable to hear of it or learn about it in the little flock of their rearing which had long since lost its heart.

If our Christology moves in this direction, so roughly sketched in these few pages, nourishing again a Christianity which refuses to cling to "the circumcisions and special diets" of a Jewish sect, my experience as a parish minister suggest that the little flock would be newly liberated to be linked to modern and international society in an open and hopeful way.

If the overarching Ephesian theme of unity guides our theological and religious thinking about Christ in this fashion, consider second, what are the implications of that same theme for the *practical* method and manner of the parish church in and for the whole world.

Does it not follow both logically and morally that, if the fullness toward which the whole creation moves is a unity in Christ, and if the church is his body and a foretaste of the Oneness which is in God, then it must demonstrate unity in its own life? The New Testament demands that we think about unity very profoundly and seriously. It pleads for a unity deeper than superimposed schemes for keeping the peace of the parish or consolidating synods. But it does not disdain the practical. So we turn now to consider the sort of unity which every little flock may well self-consciously seek in order to fulfill the divine commission and be linked to society in an open and hopeful way. We will consider two aspects of that practical unity: first, *supportive* unity, and then, *generative* unity.

The family of the flock, like the family of the flesh, is seriously compromised in its encounter with the world if it does not provide that unity within itself which is supportive to its individual members. It is beginning to dawn upon American Protestants, especially perhaps those who live in cities like New York or Chicago or in university towns like Berkeley, that we can no longer assume support in our faith from the culture around us. The disestablishment of the churches which Douglas John Hall urges [5] is already further advanced in the secular communities of my experience than his treatise suggests is widespread.

5. Douglas John Hall, *The Reality of the Gospel and the Unreality of the Churches* (Philadelphia: Westminster Press, 1975).

In one of those delightful Rabbi detective stories by Harry Kemelman, the young Rabbi visits Israel and there finds no need for the outward symbols of his faith or even to attend the synagogue, because everyone there is a Jew. In such a culture there is widespread support for the individual in his religion. Not so in our town. The campanile of a great secular university is its cathedral spire and in the interfaith council, Christians and Jews are only two of many religions represented.

During the nineteenth century, Alexis de Tocqueville, the French aristocrat, visited America expecting to find democracy a failure. To his amazement he found it working and reported his findings with an explanation. "These Americans," he said in effect, "amid all the things that divide and estrange them, have great areas in common—a common spiritual tradition, a common faith, a common scale of moral values. When they debate their differences, they debate them within the area of an undergirding and inclusive community of ideas and ideals." In this sense Christian America, if it ever was, is no more. That may be a great boon if it means that we are freed of the pretense of a Christian culture. For good or ill, it is different; and an American civil religion with its chief festival Mother's Day is no satisfactory mutation of Christianity but a heretical corruption. It is only the Gothic edition of a secular religion.

Malcolm France, writing in the London Times about being a Christian in a secular society, reminds us:

> Faith and atheism are both socially established and socially maintained. It takes a brave man to hold openly to a view of life which all his friends reject.
>
> That being the case, the churches ought to be making active preparation for supporting their members . . . in a secular society. Christianity is already being rejected by a large number of people for no better reason than that there are a large number of people who reject it.

So the little flock becomes a necessity for Christian individuals insofar as it provides that aspect of corporate unity which is supportive to persons one by one. I really do not know for sure who Principal Denny was—only that he is some Scot educator or theologian canonized in Presbyterian sermon illustrations for years—but in one such story he was asked how he endured so well the public abuse to which he was subjected and he is reported to have replied that he could endure because he was happy at home. That is a very obliging response for our purpose here because it suggests some of the resources needed to be found in the little flock in order for it corporately and through its members to be linked helpfully and hopefully to society at large.

But disclaimers must be entered at once. We are not talking about that superficial unity which is an accommodation of convictions in order to get along on the surface. No natural family is strong in that fashion and no reading of Ephesians suggests any such pragmatic unity. Unity which arises out of a common allegiance to Christ and a personal loyalty to Jesus brings with it the balance and the support and the questioning and the health which come from diverse gifts and separate but not separating points of view.

Not long ago an articulate, intelligent, and aggressively conservative member of our little flock spoke to me most warmly about another member. I was a bit surprised because, so far as I know, they have disagreed on every political and social issue that has come along— Vietnam, migrant labor, rent control, amnesty, criminal justice. I pointed that fact out to him and he replied, "Of course we disagree but we can talk together because we have the same starting place. I always listen to him because I know we share the same faith. I sense he feels the same way about me!" That mutual respect always means very productive encounters.

There is a footnote which I feel constrained to enter at this juncture because the supportive aspect of unity is not a matter of concern only to the inward life of the local church, although that is the point of our emphasis. We need the supportive aspect of unity desperately throughout *all* the various manifestations of the church. This is a grave practical matter in our time when mutual suspicion is driving wedges between parts of the church. We could use some of that productivity which mutual respect, even between disagreeing parties, can produce. The scandal of local churches which presume independence from one another and from the theological schools and councils and assemblies of the whole church is matched only by the scandal of such theological schools and councils and their officers and members separating themselves from the experiential center of Christian faith, the surrounding body of the worshiping community.

However, if we search out only that aspect of unity which provides a support system for individual Christians and for the various agencies of the church, we may well end up with a closed system and a church without warmth and life and growing edges. Someone has said that to bring a new Christian into some of our churches today is like putting a fully hatched chick under a dead hen. So enough now of *supportive* unity. Let us turn to consider another aspect of unity, which we have elected to call *generative* unity.

A natural world in which new life springs out of the unity of male and female, the unity of the diverse, is a singular lesson for the church. If the unity which is in Christ is to be revealed in a new humanity through the discourse and dialogue of persons and cultures with diverse gifts and experience, how much more immediate is the promise of the generative power of unity in the little flock. That creative possibility lies at the heart of every conflict in the church and insistently demands that we open ourselves to its emergent power.

However, there is in the land a popular model of ministry which effectively blocks the generative power of unity. It is a model which suggests that the prophetic role of both pulpit and council is rooted in such profound and special understanding of the implication of the eternal verities in every issue which arises that to question the prophet or not to sign the latest petition or resolution is a subtle maneuver of the devil. Andrew Greeley, who frequently overstates his case, nevertheless has a point when he writes in *Theology Today:*

I confess that I look in vain for any such self-doubt in most of the political and liberation theologians. They are so certain of themselves and their world view that they simply cannot admit that something might be learned from other perspectives, from empirical research, from international economics, or even from the people they are so determined to convert and liberate. A word of caution, a note of uncertainty, an admission of the possibility of error, a vague concession to greyness—where does one find this. . . . When does one hear a political theologian concede that human reality is so complex and so obscure that no policy, no pro-

gram can possibly be so self-evidently correct that all Christians are com-
pelled to accept it without question or debate? [6]

Many of us who may have a high degree of resistance to Greeley, the
priest-columnist, will nonetheless listen to Reinhold Niebuhr, the
pastor-professor-prophet who warned years ago, "as soon as the Protestant assumes that his more prophetic statement and interpretation of
the Christian Gospel guarantees him a superior virtue, he is also lost
in the sin of self-righteousness." [7]

Undue certainty and any self-righteousness about the implications
of Christian faith is not a very promising approach to an open and
hopeful relationship with society outside the church and it is a great
obstacle to the generative power of unity within the church. We are
speaking of that kind of unity which provides breathing space for persons of very different views and experience to come together for the
revealing and growth which conversation in Christ's name and under
the discipline of the Scriptures can produce. We have had within the
year such conversations in our congregation on amnesty and on criminal justice. The effort in these conversations and others like them is
not to hack out some Christian consensus or get some majority vote by
which we presume God's will is determined and revealed. It is not to
win a few more votes for our point of view or to convince our neighbor
of his outrageous stupidity or infidelity to Christ because he does not
agree with us. Rather, it is to invite the creative power present in
Christian unity to be active and productive in our midst and direct us
in our discussions and future actions.

In Christ we are set free to come and reason together, assured that
there is "yet more light to break forth from God's holy word" on the
immediate and pressing life-and-death issues of the modern world. Its
concern is not so much conclusions but a process which opens to God's
conclusions; it is the work of creating out of chaos, the generative
power which unity supplies at the heart of diversity and conflict.

6. January 1974, p. 396.
7. *The Nature and Destiny of Man* (New York: Charles Scribner's Sons, 1947), vol. I,
p. 202.

So we believe that more and more congregations may become rein-vigorating communities of faith to more and more persons as they open themselves to be discovered by that unity which is in Christ and which is both supportive and generative. If the community of Chris-tian faith is to be linked to the whole world in an open and hopeful way, it will need with much prayer and wisdom to incorporate into the fabric of its life the overarching theme of unity put forth so long ago to that little flock in Ephesus. Such unity will expand its under-standing of and its relationship to the Eternal Christ; and it will also provide support and energy for its mission in the world.

So it seems to move of necessity back and forth in substantial in-terchange between the doctrinal or theological and the practical or methodological. But so be it, we are in good company, for the letter to the Ephesians was also so divided. You will remember, however, that squarely in the midst of the epistle, the first highly doctrinal chapters and the following practical earthy chapters are tied together with a magnificent confession:

> For this reason I bow my knees before the Father from whom every fam-ily in heaven and on earth is named. . . .

So again, as for centuries past, the distinctive quality of life in the church emerges quite in contrast to the many secular alternative com-munities blooming and dying around us. It appears when two or three or many hundreds come together in the unity which Christ supplies and bow the knee before the Father from whom every family—Arab, Christian, Jew—every tribe, every race, every nation, is named. Then *with* Christ and *through* Christ the church enters openly and hopefully into the world around it with the only power it truly derives from God, the power to suffer, because in him it is led into the pain of the world, into its separation and anguish, into fear and trouble.

Thus the everlasting difference between Christ's little flock and all other communities is revealed: the difference of a symbol and the dif-ference of a language; and the symbol is the cross and the language is prayer. Thus the Christ of the cosmos becomes the Christ of the heart; and through its corporate prayer in the name and spirit of its crucified and risen Lord, the little flock participates at once in that unity and beauty which will one day mark the new heaven and the new earth where God dwells with his people and where the whole creation dances together in unity and in joy.

Appendix A:
Sunburst

A detailed account of Sunburst prepared by
Mary K. Stiles, one of the sector leaders,
in response to inquiries about that program

First Congregational Church of Berkeley (FCCB) is located on the doorstep of the University of California. It ministers to a group of over thirteen hundred persons who are living within a radius of twenty miles.

After one of our associate ministers resigned, a Leadership Review Committee reviewed our pastoral needs. They recommended that personnel be found "to coordinate and develop with staff, appropriate boards and the congregation, continuous and expanded programs of evangelism, membership, stewardship, and the nurture of members of the congregation by each other."

Subsequently a Pastoral Search Committee proposed that this intention might be carried out more effectively by a corps of lay volunteers than by a single person. Their plan was:

1. that the parish shall be designated in sectors, possibly six in number, and that a core caring center in each sector would provide occasion for worship and communion in local settings and help the persons in the sector to "walk together in Christian love and sym-

pathy" in concrete and specific ways in keeping with the promise
we have made to each other;

2. that the ministry of the caring centers would be encouraged and
   enabled through sector leaders;

3. that these six sector leaders together with the ministers would con-
   stitute the central coordinating core. As such they would meet
   weekly for prayer, reporting, planning, and consultation;

4. that the program be known as "Sunburst."

These steps toward establishment of the program were suggested:
(1) recruitment (6 weeks); (2) design (6 weeks); (3) preparation of sector leaders (6 weeks).

RECRUITMENT

The proposal was approved by the congregation at a church meeting
on January 13, and in the next two weekly issues of our newsletter,
The Carillon, the following classified advertisement appeared:

WANTED

FCCB is ready to engage, without salary, lead workers for Sunburst.
Time commitment: not less than 20 hours a week. Such volunteers must
be open to receive appropriate instruction and guidance which will be
commensurate with the responsibility to be assumed. They must be persons who have the potential to help others in groups and individually.
They must be physically mobile. They must be readily accessible by telephone. They must be open to growth and change themselves and have
the ability to relate warmly to others. They will be reimbursed for expenses incurred, such as travel, telephone, supplementary education. . . .

By the end of March six volunteers had been duly interviewed and
screened. All were women in the "middle" years; five had reared or
were rearing families who had grown up in the church, all had been
involved in voluntary or professional teaching roles and had carried
heavy responsibilties in community outreach. Together they had a
combined total of 118 years of FCCB membership. Each made a commitment of two years; there were no signed contracts.

On March 31 they were introduced to the congregation by way of

The Carillon, which published their pictures and brief biographical sketches.

RELATIONSHIP OF SUNBURST TEAM TO PAID STAFF

By April 2 an office with telephone was established in the church. The total Sunburst team was to consist of the senior minister, the youth minister, a church secretary, the six sector leaders, and the associate minister, who was to act as convener. Six months later a woman who had been a long-time lay assistant and parish visitor was invited to join the team during periods when member concerns were being considered.

DESIGN

Meetings of the entire team were scheduled on a weekly basis, to be held for two and one half hours on a weekday morning for the first three months. The meeting format: opening devotions and prayer; study (fifty-minute seminar); business and announcements; reporting by sectors—sharing of concerns, needs, and accomplishments.

Additionally Sunburst leaders met as a group of six, usually for one to two hours weekly, and each leader was also assigned one staff minister with whom she could consult privately for one hour weekly. The latter became known as "tutorial" sessions.

The total team of ten has continued its meetings on a weekly basis, fifty-two weeks of the year, but has decreased the time to one and one-half hours; tutorials still exist at the discretion of the Sunburst leaders.

All of the original six leaders are still involved and one part-time assistant has been added to the corps. She absorbs part of the load of one sector leader who finds the time commitment rather heavy.

PREPARATION AND TRAINING

Preparation is an ongoing process, just as is the educational process at FCCB. During the first May and June three seminars were offered exclusively for Sunburst leaders:

1. *Bible Study: The Synoptic Gospels*—four sessions. Leader: Dr. Barr. Text: W. D. Davis, *Invitation to the New Testament;*
2. *The Theology of Person*—six sessions. Leader: Rev. Mary Eakin. Based on the trilogy of I, Other, and God in relationship;
3. *The Group Process*—six sessions. Leader: Rev. Al Kissling. Skills for leaders and participants. Text: Robert Leslie, *Sharing Groups in the Church.*

During September:

Value Clarification—four sessions. Leader: Rev. Al Kissling. Text: Sid Simon, *Value Clarification.*

In addition, Sunburst leaders took advantage of the ongoing educational curriculum offered by the ministerial staff. At least one, and often more, of the leaders attended the following:

1. June–July   Seven sessions on discussion of *The Simple Life* by Vernard Eller. Mary Eakin, Leader;

2. June–July   Four sessions on *The Gospel of Mark*. Mary Eakin, Leader.

3. August   Four sessions on discussion of *Dance of the Pilgrim* by John D. McGuire. Laurella Bonifazi, Lay Leader;

4. August   Four *"Sermon Seminars"* on the subject of "Jesus and the American Scene," based on the four gospels. Dr. Barr, Leader. Designed to elicit interest, suggestions, and feelings of participation in preparation of the next Sunday's sermon;

5.   Two weekends—*Spiritual Renewal Workshop.* Dr. Howard Fuller, Leader and minister member of FCCB. This developed into an ongoing Meditation/Discussion/Support group of twelve participants and has met continuously every other week for two hours, with plans to continue into another year. Three Sunburst leaders are members of the group;

6. October–   Six sessions on *The Helping Relationship* by Lawrence M. December   Brammer. Mary Eakin, Leader.

7. Lenten
Season
Six weeks of study centered on the development of UCC's Statement of Faith and the meaning of our own Covenant. Organized geographically in sectors and led by ministers and trained laypersons.

8. July
Worship/Sermon Seminars—designed and led by Dr. Barr for preparation of leadership for implementing his concept of "Owning the Worship Service." These meetings continue in units of three successive weeks, rotating them through each one of the sectors. By the end of six months members in each sector have had the opportunity to participate in one 3-week workshop involved in worship and sermon preparation;

9. October–
November
Eleven sessions—*To Love as Jesus Loved* (reflections on and response to the Gospel of John). Mary Eakin, Leader.

SUPPLEMENTARY LEADERSHIP PREPARATION

Several books have come to our attention as being particularly helpful. Among them are: Robert Raines, *New Life in the Church;* Charles Shedd, *The Pastoral Ministry of Church Officers;* Granger E. Westberg, *Good Grief.*

The Pacific School of Religion in Berkeley also offers opportunities in short workshops designed for lay leadership participation. One such intensive two-week workshop on alcoholism was attended by two Sunburst leaders during the summer, and several one-day workshops during the school year were attended by others.

Retreats arranged exclusively for the total Sunburst Team proved to be helpful in sorting out priorities, problems, and frustrations: (1) a full-day session, out of town, during our "Design" period of the first of April; (2) a six-hour retreat held at the conclusion of our June preparation period, at which time we were ready to launch intensive visitations of sector members; (3) a six-hour retreat at the completion of our first year, designed for evaluation of the task so far and discussion of future expectations.

SUMMARY OF GOALS, ACCOMPLISHMENTS, AND PROBLEMS

A. Goals:
1. To grow together spiritually; creating a community of encouragement and increasing biblical and theological knowledge.
2. To develop technical skills of calling and communicating; to learn detachment, listening, and reflection; to exploit opportunities rather than becoming problem oriented; to move out from the center.
3. To function as caring and channeling individuals, not as programmers.
4. To build on individual strengths in our own unique ways; to set personal goals for improvement; and to avoid any feelings of competitiveness among the sectors.

B. Accomplishments:
1. Within the first year each leader felt that she knew, at some level, probably ninety per cent of her sector members; while deeper, more meaningful relationships had been developed with perhaps an average of fifty per cent. Contact had been made with the remaining ten per cent but the level of communication was still low or non-existent.
2. Members seemed to be developing deeper feelings and concerns for others, new channels of communication were opening, and seemingly more persons could share with circles of increasing size.
3. Some "lost" members had been found and there was less anxiety about neglected and lonely persons. A "Traveling Road Show" on problems peculiar to, or intensified by, aging had been developed. One sector had organized a taxi pool to assist nondriving church members to attend church on Sundays.
4. At the present time within each sector various types of assistants have emerged; e.g., homes are continually being offered as gathering places for small coffee hours, teas, luncheons, and dinners; men and women are offering limited time to assist or

accompany leaders on home visitations; others are assisting by telephone calling, offering secretarial skills, etc.

5. There is an expressed, but immeasurable, sense of individual personal growth among members and a definitely increased level of lay identity.

6. Some of the sector leaders and their "caring coordinators" have become involved in neighborhood Discipleship Groups in which new members are oriented and nurtured for three successive weeks immediately subsequent to their joining the church.

C. Problems:

1. Finding valid and reliable means of evaluating progress and accomplishments.

2. Keeping "fresh," optimistic, and free of guilt for not moving as speedily as envisioned.

3. Developing between leaders and members a viable "helping" relationship that was one of enabling and developing responsibility and self-direction, rather that one of problem solving, directing, or supervising.

4. Clarifying role as confidante; knowing when and how to refer problems to team or ministerial staff.

5. Seeking methods of increasing the involvement of male members.

6. Establishing a "Caring Core" by drawing leadership from within each neighborhood of each sector.

During the first year it was inevitable that we should suffer periods of frustrations and instances of interpersonal misunderstandings. Once we experimented briefly with a "Commitment Group." For six weeks the six sector leaders met together for prayer, support, and conversation, using Thomas R. Kelly's *A Testament of Devotion.* We worked through a crisis, and after vacations and periods of grief for two leaders who lost family members we found ourselves more harmoniously united than ever and looking forward to another year for Sunburst.

CHRONOLOGY OF EVENTS

| March through December | Leadership Review and Pastoral Search Committee work. |

January	"Sunburst" design recommended and approved at church meeting by congregation.
March	Recruitment complete. Sunburst leaders introduced to congregation.
April	First formal meeting of Sunburst Team (ten members, including staff).
April	Full-day retreat of Sunburst Team to work on goals, purposes, and design.
May	Progress report of Sunburst described at Sunday church meeting. Area map of proposed sector divisions presented. Stated goal: "To walk together in Christian love and sympathy." A Sunburst design encircled by the following words and phrases was explained:

Fellowship	Warmth	Creating
Rekindling	Growing	Praise
Sharing	Joy	Radiating
Caring	Challenging	

Responsive	Ministering Congregation
Accepting	Enabling
Listening	Covenanting Community
Nurturing	Good News

June	Second full-day retreat to plan activities program.
June	Membership Sunday. *The Carillon* carried sectors map and listed leaders; each sector met separately after church service for a "get-acquainted" Coffee Hour. Posters containing pictures of members and name tags were prepared.
June	Intensive visiting in sectors began; sector leaders organized lists of members and divided each sector into eight or ten neighborhoods.

July–August	Small meetings in homes arranged with purpose of increasing awareness of neighborhood membership.
September	Individual Sunburst stationery with logo and Scripture prepared.
October	Intensive home visiting slowed down to accommodate Stewardship Drive, which involved neighborhood meetings.
October	Sunburst (leaders only) all-day evaluation/discussion.
November	Church centennial dinner celebration. Sunburst leaders encouraged widespread participation—car pools, etc., for sector members.
April	Completion of Sunburst's first year. All-day retreat for evaluation—attended by total Sunburst Team.
July–August	After-church Coffee Hour for each sector on successive Sundays.
September	Plans made for rotation through sectors of "Owning the Service" seminars; each sector to sponsor three successive weeks.
September	Plans in making for Stewardship meetings to be held in homes within each sector. Sunburst cooperates with Board of Stewardship but takes care to avoid confusion with Stewardship.

Appendix B:
The Case of the
Pregnant School Teacher

The following sermon "Miss Harriet's Baby" is based on a case drawn from a newspaper report. Every member of the sermon seminar was provided with the entire newspaper clipping but the case presented serious practical limitations. Such reports are skimpy and often sensationalized; details are not known and the discussion could ramble all around, as every person supplies conditions to his own liking. Probably case studies of this sort are of doubtful value except that they are current and lively and in the public concern at the time.

Recognizing some of the built-in problems, the leader of the seminar which studied this case persuaded the group to decide arbitrarily on some assumptions to narrow the field. They were as follows:

Harriet Wardlaw is a competent teacher.

By custom, if married, she wouldn't be transferred when pregnant.

She and J. Cox have been living together as a couple for one and one half years.

They have a yearly contract.

They may or may not stay together indefinitely.

As it developed, these limiting assumptions did not prove crucial and may have handicapped the discussion more than they helped. It did alert the seminar to the dangers of having too little information.

The decision of the judge was known to the seminar and to many members of the congregation at the time the case was before us. So that material from the newspaper was also included in the case.

SERMON: Miss Harriet's Baby

New Testament Lesson: John 7:53–8:11, Jesus and the Woman Taken in Adultery.
Text: Exodus 20:14, "You shall not commit adultery."

Harriet Wardlaw is an unmarried twenty-nine-year-old woman school teacher in Austin, Texas. She recently became newsworthy when she brought a lawsuit against the Superintendent of Schools. She charged discrimination because he transferred her from a classroom position after she told school officials she was pregnant. The sermon seminar uncovered many possible issues in this case study: sex discrimination, the role of teachers as instructors in morality, their position as character models, the rights of a woman about her own body, the effect upon a child of a single parent—even the question of ministers or school teachers smoking in public! There was no general agreement about which commandment applied most pertinently to the case of Miss Harriet and her baby. "Thou shalt not covet," was suggested, as was "Honor thy father and thy mother." Others thought the commandment about "false witness" should be considered.

As we have seen repeatedly during these weeks spent with the Ten Commandments, they have a magnificent unity and the first five especially all bear in some way on all matters of human conduct. However, partly not to disappoint some members of this congregation, but more because it gets to the central concern in Miss Harriet's case, I propose as our text today the Seventh Commandment, "Thou shalt not commit adultery." Strictly speaking Miss Harriet had not committed adultery. The father of her baby is not currently married and so on these purely technical grounds adultery is not involved, for in the Old Testament that term is used exclusively for marital infidelity.

But the Ten Commandments are guidelines, not definitions, and her deliberately planned pregnancy with no intention of marriage is a declared lifestyle in direct contradiction to the teachings of the Scripture and the tradition of the church. If it is a protest against that tradition and that teaching, it is in no way an isolated protest. Miss Harriet is no exception. She has many sympathizers in and out of this congregation. Berkeley teachers, the sermon seminar was told, are pressing for a clause in their new contract to provide maternity benefits for unmarried teachers. So it appears crucial that we consider the commandment forbidding adultery because in its original setting the primary concern of that commandment was to protect the integrity of the marriage relationship.

This commandment is the most specific of the ten in continuing the tradition which views the absolute commitment of two persons to each other as the foundation stone of Christian marriage. That lifetime covenant between a woman and a man involves the mutual exchange of self to the trust and keeping of another person in a unique, personal, sexual, and social relationship, without any reservations or escape clauses, "to love, comfort, honor and keep . . . so long as ye both shall live." When you hear even in a conservative church, one which makes particular *claims* to biblical faithfulness, a marriage service in which the phrase "so long as ye both shall live" is replaced with the phrase, "for the duration of this relationship," you begin to sense how deep is the erosion of the concept of Christian marriage.

I firmly believe that the church must clearly and intelligently reaffirm the teaching that every child needs both male and female parent equally, and encourage marriage where commitment takes priority over romance and the welfare of society is considered of equal importance to the personal happiness of the individual parties involved. If Christian people are to bear this witness and strengthen one another in living it, and if they are to be a creative influence in the thoughtful review of marriage in our time, that witness will need to be constantly corrected and tempered and enhanced by five complementary emphases to which I invite your thoughtful reflection and response.

First, it will be a witness borne with compassion and without condemnation. In the New Testament Lesson today, Jesus upheld the law about adultery. So also his church must uphold every effort to keep marriage unadulterated, to preserve it from being weakened or made impure and inferior, from missing the beauty and vigor it can possess. But, while upholding this ideal by not condoning adultery, Jesus also showed compassion for the troubled woman.

For years I have felt this sermon should be preached in *this* pulpit, in *this* city, in *this* state, but I have postponed it because I have lacked heart. One Sunday I did a rough calculation and discovered scarcely a pew in this sanctuary, upstairs or down, where there was not some person hurting terribly for himself or for one he loves from the breakdown of a marriage, or where there was not another person, perhaps in even more poignant sorrow, so tangled by childhood fears or crushed by adolescent trauma that he or she had been cheated from the fullness of this profoundly personal relationship. No word on this subject is appropriate unless it is at once a word of compassion and understanding and love. Who is there who wants to throw the first stone or even the last where the cuts are still bleeding and the bruises will be tender until the Great Assize? When Jesus asked that question about who would throw the first stone, it was reported that it was the oldest persons in the gathering who slinked off first. That scene should not escape the attention of those of us who are the oldest in our society and our congregation and who are most firmly established in tradition and who are often the most vocal in criticism of the changing marriage arrangements of the younger generation. Let him who is without sin— without complicity—throw the first stone. "And they went away, one by one, beginning with the eldest." So, compassion first!

Second, the Christian witness for marriage as a contract of integrity and permanence will be a witness which will work for change. This second emphasis we will label adaptation without adulteration. The play on words is appropriate. We need to respond to the changing scene with changing forms of marriage which do not adulterate the divine purpose of personal and social unity and health. Many a marriage has been adulterated far worse by some hard, unloving, unforgiving person than by his or her legally unfaithful partner. One objection to Miss Harriet's scheme to have a baby all on her own, so to speak, is the psychological effect of the totally absent father. But many a legally faithful husband is absent from his wife and child in such a way as to make them think that Miss Harriet has a pretty good idea after all! At least she *expects* nothing of the father.

So this second emphasis is *adaptation without adulteration.* The Israelites adapted their laws and customs to changing circumstances, to the loss of nationality, to the disintegration of the exile, to their fuller exposure to other cultures. So in a time of "the pill" and the passing of an agrarian economy where children were an economic asset there must come inevitable adaptations in marriage, discarding rigid and outdated male-female roles and replacing scattered *natural* families with loving *gathered* families and experimenting with surrogate parents and grandparents and compensating for the disappearance of the village or clan with new smaller groups of parish or neighborhood or Christian commune. All kinds of new forms and styles must be encouraged to emerge and develop in a new and different age, but the guidelines are given to permit *adaptation—without adulteration.*

All through the Scripture there is the record of a people struggling together—sometimes they are in a matriarchal society, more often it is patriarchal; sometimes a stern and rigid society, permitting divorce only for infidelity, sometimes a more permissive society, allowing divorce for such trivia as burned bread; but never did that society abandon the conviction that the relationships between the sexes was a concern of faith. They saw sexuality related to God's creative purposes and to be fulfilled best within the context of an extraordinary personal and public commitment.

This brings us squarely to the *third emphasis* in Christian witness about Christian marriage. *Such witness will seek to make clear that Christians are concerned about commitment in marriage because marriage is a social contract with vast public dimensions.* This is immediately clear in Miss Harriet's case. Her pregnancy is an embarrassment to the school administration because it is not strictly a personal affair no matter how earnestly she declares that it is.

Professor Stanley Coopersmith at the Davis Campus of the University of California has conducted studies which lead him to believe that contemporary young people in our society tend to regard marriage and divorce as *personal* concerns whereas their parents tend to believe they are *social* concerns. This is interesting in light of the usual idealistic and appropriate concern of young people for social justice. They might be surprised by studies which show, according to George Gilder, that "the real arenas of 'sexual revolution' in America are not the universities but the black ghettos. . . . But the ghetto does not provide a secure place for the losers." [1] The real losers in the adulteration of marriage in American life include many who are already otherwise handicapped by society and by vast inequities of opportunity.

Gilder makes a further observation about Open Marriage that is not frequently heard in the fashionable clubs and churches, but is painfully and conspicuously experienced by many a man or woman who has been the victim of our liberation from commitment in marriage. He writes: ". . . the removal of restrictions on sexual activity does not bring equality and community. It brings ever more vicious sexual competition. The women become 'easier' for the powerful to get, but harder for others to keep. Divorces become 'easier,' but remarriage is extremely difficult for abandoned older women. Marriages become more 'open'—open not only for the partners to get out but also for the powerful to get in." That happens in the sophisticated levels of this community; it also happens in the deprived levels of this community. And in both places the result is not only personal dislocation and grief but a tearing at a social fabric which has and can make possible a secure and decent community for Miss Harriet's baby when it arrives—even without a father.

We must move on now and note that marriage is not only a public matter; it is also a very personal matter. Mark then as a *fourth emphasis* in the witness of the church just this: *that the fulfillment of the personal promise in marriage also desperately calls for commitment by both parties.* Such a complex, involved, changing relationship as marriage is, with its intimacies and its strains and its public involvement and its inclusion of new and unpredictable personalities in children with their gifts and struggles—how any such relationship can thrive and grow and be a thing of beauty year upon year seems to me virtually impossible under the insecurities of the rubric that our promises to each other are valid only for "the duration of this relationship." Indeed, a marriage

1. George Gilder, "In Defense of Monogamy" in *Commentary* (Nov. 1974).

may only come into its own and truly blossom with its potential when it is only the commitment they feel that requires a couple to keep on working at it even when they don't want to do so. I believe in divorce; I believe the church must sometimes encourage divorce—to end a youthful mistake or declare dead a relationship long past resuscitation and to give a person a fresh beginning, but to marry with tongue in cheek and reservations in heart and divorce in mind is hardly Christian marriage!

Some present attempts to revise the traditional marriage service seem to me most appropriate. I have never heard or spoken the word "obey" in the marriage service and I refuse to cite St. Paul, as does the Book of Common Prayer, for I fear that he was not an expert in marital arrangements. But one biblical phrase which many young persons wish removed from the service is another matter. It is related to Genesis 2:24–25: "Therefore a man shall leave his father and his mother, and shall cleave unto his wife; and they shall be one flesh. And they were both naked, the man and his wife, and were not ashamed." A service recently publicized within the Northern California Conference of the United Church of Christ, to which we belong, includes these words: "While a man and a woman have traditionally become 'one,' so to speak, a new and more healthy outlook is being taken—an outlook which affirms the unique importance and life of both parties to the contract. No longer do two become 'one.' " [2]

Christian marriage is helped whenever the church repudiates the idea, not uncommon in Scripture and tradition, that marriage is a matter of a woman giving up her identity to a man. But the concept of becoming "one" when properly traced to its biblical roots involves no such distortion of personhood, but rather, its fulfillment. Becoming "one" points to that ideal completion and wholeness of existence which in Christian myth and legend woman and man possessed before the Fall. They were not ashamed. As Gerhard von Rad has written: "That inexplicable split in human nature did not yet exist," that disturbance of inward harmony and peace had not yet possessed personhood.

The "oneness" which is therefore the ideal toward which marriage is

2. Task Force on Women in Church and Society, NCC, UCC, Winter 1974.

directed is the restoration of that personal harmony and peace. But that harmony and that peace are misunderstood if they are described as the absence of conflict. Indeed, conflict itself is the instrument of each new level of that oneness, that wholeness of being. In a thoughtful book on *The Concept of Peace,* John Macquarrie describes its dynamics in terms of conflict. Jesus said he had come not to bring peace but a sword, and "conflict," claims Macquarrie, "must be included within wholeness. A wholeness which does not include conflict is a frozen condition, a kind of death lacking dynamism and the possibility of new development."

Marriage without conflict is marriage without a growing edge; it is a marriage which has compromised its future. But my experience suggests that without commitment the possibility of creative, dynamic conflict is seriously endangered. When conflict arises in marriage, even the ultimate personal conflict of a new infatuation as well as conflict over money, children, or variations in basal metabolism, without commitment we tend then to take the easier way out, of dissolution rather than resolution, of icy separation rather than painful communication.

Now this sermon has grown much too long and you may well wonder if we are going on now seriously to a fifth point. Yes, we are—but in a sense we are going to spend all the Sundays in Lent on it. That *fifth emphasis* is: *that the potential as well as the witness of Christian marriage cannot be managed alone* but in the company of a supporting cast of forgiven and forgiving persons who have committed themselves in a more comprehensive covenant with one another and with the God of All Being, a community of persons devoutly open for possession by the indwelling Christ, the forerunner of the new humanity.

So, as we close this study of the commandments and turn to the Lenten reflection on covenant, we remember in Christian marriage and in all other expressions and experiences of Christian community the testimony in Ephesians to the Christ who "is our peace, who has made us both one, and has broken down the dividing wall of hostility, by abolishing in his flesh the law of commandments so as to create . . . a single new humanity in himself, thereby making peace." [3]

3. Ephesians 2 (adapted from RSV and NEB).